Html5

Learn Html and Css With a Complete Tutorial
Guide

*(The Fifth and Current Major Version of the
Html Standard)*

Shawn Catlett

Published By **Tayson Maxwell**

Shawn Catlett

Html5: Learn Html and Css With a Complete Tutorial Guide (The Fifth and Current Major Version of the Html Standard)

ISBN   978-1-77485-514-0

Legal & Disclaimer

The information contained in this ebook is not designed to replace or take the place of any form of medicine or professional medical advice. The information in this ebook has been provided for educational & entertainment purposes only.

The information contained in this book has been compiled from sources deemed reliable, and it is accurate to the best of the Author's knowledge; however, the Author cannot guarantee its accuracy and validity and cannot be held liable for any errors or omissions. Changes are periodically made to this book. You must consult your doctor or get professional medical advice before using any of the suggested remedies, techniques, or information in this book.

Upon using the information contained in this book, you agree to hold harmless the Author from and against any damages, costs, and expenses, including any legal fees potentially resulting from the application of any of the

TABLE OF CONTENTS

Introduction

As a beginner, it is a logical assumption to think that HTML5 is simply the fifth version of the HTML web page-writing language. You will be surprised to learn that it is much more. HTML5 takes a completely new turn and helps developers correct their markup mistakes rather than simply rejecting. It also makes it possible to play videos without a browser plug-in (think Flash).

It allows users to give their websites the same interactive capabilities seen in traditional desktop software, through the use of JavaScript-fueled features.

This book is intended for beginners. Those who have experience in web page design and programming will find this book to be overly simple. On the flip side, this will be a perfect immersion to those completely new to this game. Together we will:

Take a moment to learn about the World Wide Web
What it takes to plan and create a website

Then we will jump in by creating your very first webpage. While it won't win any design awards, it will allow you to see firsthand the elements and features of an HTML5 web-page. In creating your first webpage we will learn:

What HTML5 Is and Its Benefits
Finding out the importance of an HTML tag
Understanding an HTML Document
Once we have covered the basics, we will focus on various simple text elements and formatting which will allow you to create easily readable text. We will learn:

Paragraphs
Headings
Line Breaks
Lines
All about lists
Tables
Inline Formatting
The focus of this Book is to help you understand basic skills, you will not learn how to become a professional web designer just by reading this book. It will, however, teach you the general principles that will help you launch into this new and exciting world of web page design. Follow along with the numerous examples, and practice creating your own HTML documents, and soon you will be proficient at creating webpages using HTML.

Chapter 1: Getting Started With Html

Version	Specification	Release	Date
1.0	N/A		1994-01-01
2.0	RFC	1866	1995-11-24
3.2	W3C: HTML 3.2 Specification		1997-01-14
4.0	W3C: HTML 4.0 Specification		1998-04-24
4.01	W3C: HTML 4.01 Specification		1999-12-24
5	WHATWG: HTML Living Standard		2014-10-28
5.1	W3C: HTML 5.1 Specification		2016-11-01

Section 1.1: Hello World
Introduction

HTML (**H**ypertext **M**arkup **L**anguage) uses a markup system composed of elements which represent specific content. *Markup* means that with HTML you declare *what* is presented to a viewer, not *how* it is presented. Visual representations are defined by Cascading Style Sheets (CSS) and realized by browsers. Still existing elements that allow for such, like e.g. font, "are entirely obsolete, and must not be used by authors"[1].

HTML is sometimes called a programming language but it has no logic, so is a **markup language**. HTML tags provide semantic meaning and machine-readability to the content in the page.

An element usually consists of an opening tag (**<element_name>**), a closing tag (**</element_name>**), which contain the element's name surrounded by angle brackets, and the content in between: **<element_name>**...content...**</element_name>**

There are some HTML elements that don't have a closing tag or any contents. These are called void elements. Void elements include **<img>**, **<meta>**, **<link>** and **<input>**. Element names can be thought of as descriptive keywords for the content they contain, such as video, audio, table, footer. A HTML page may consist of potentially hundreds of elements which are then read by a web browser, interpreted and rendered into human readable or audible content on the screen.

For this document it is important to note the difference between elements and tags:
Elements:video, audio, table, footer
Tags:<video>, **<audio>**, **<table>**, **<footer>**, **</html>**, **</body>**
Element **insight**
Let's break down a tag...
The **<p>** tag represents a common paragraph.

Elements commonly have an opening tag and a closing tag. The opening tag contains the element's name in angle brackets (**<p>**). The closing tag is identical to the opening tag with the addition of a forward slash (/) between the opening bracket and the element's name (**</p>**).

Content can then go between these two tags: **<p>**This is a simple paragraph.**</p>**.
Creating a simple page
The following HTML example creates a simple "Hello World" web page. HTML files can be created using any text editor. The files must be saved with a .html or .htm[2] extension in order to be recognized as HTML files.

Once created, this file can be opened in any web browser.

<!DOCTYPE html> **<html** lang="en"**>**

<head>
<meta charset="UTF-8"**> <title>**Hello!**</title>**

</head>

<body>
<h1>Hello World!**</h1>**
<p>This is a simple paragraph.**</p>**

</body>
</html>

Simple   page   break   down
These are the tags used in the example:

Tag   **Meaning**

<!DOCTYPE
>

Defines the HTML version used in the
document. In this case it is HTML5.
See the doctypes topic for more information.

Opens the page. No markup should come after
the closing tag (**</html>**). The lang attribute
declares **<html>** the primary language of the page
using the ISO language codes (en for English).
See the Content Language topic for more
information.

Opens the head section, which does not appear in
the main browser window but mainly contains
<head> information *about* the HTML document,
called *metadata*. It can also contain imports from
external
stylesheets and scripts. The closing tag is
</head>.

Gives the browser some metadata about the
document. The charset attribute declares the
character **<meta>**

encoding . Modern HTML documents should
always use UTF-8, even though it is not a
requirement. In HTML, the **<meta>** tag does not

require   a   closing   tag.
See the Meta topic for more information.

The title of the page. Text written between this
opening and the closing tag (**</title>**) will
be_{**<title>**} displayed on the tab of the page or in the title bar of the
browser.
Opens the part of the document displayed to
users, i.e. all the visible or audible content of a
page. No_{**<body>**} content should be added after the closing tag
</body>.
<h1>
A   level   1   heading   for   the   page.
See   headings   for   more   information.   **<p>**
Represents   a   common   paragraph   of   text.
1. ↑ HTML5, 11.2 Non-conforming features
2. ↑.htm is inherited from the legacy DOS
three character file extension limit.

Chapter 2: Doctypes

Doctypes - short for 'document type' - help
browsers to understand the version of HTML the
document is written in for better interpretability.
Doctype declarations are not HTML tags and
belong at the very top of a document. This topic
explains the structure and declaration of various
doctypes in HTML.

Section 2.1: Adding the Doctype

The <!DOCTYPE> declaration should always be included at the top of the HTML document, before the **<html>** tag.
Version ≥ 5
See HTML 5 Doctype for details on the HTML 5 Doctype.
<!DOCTYPE html>

Section 2.2: HTML 5 Doctype
HTML5 is not based on SGML (Standard Generalized Markup Language), and therefore does not require a reference to a DTD (Document Type Definition).
HTML 5 Doctype declaration:
<!DOCTYPE html>
Case Insensitivity
Per the W3.org HTML 5 DOCTYPE Spec:
A DOCTYPE must consist of the following components, in this order:
1. A string that is an ASCII **case-insensitive** match for the string "<!DOCTYPE".
therefore the following DOCTYPEs are also valid:

<!doctype html > <!dOCtyPe html> <!DocTYpe html>

This SO article discusses the topic extensively:
Uppercase or lowercase doctype?

Chapter 3: Headings

HTML provides not only plain paragraph tags, but six separate header tags to indicate headings of various sizes and thicknesses. Enumerated as heading 1 through heading 6, heading 1 has the largest and thickest text while heading 6 is the smallest and thinnest, down to the paragraph level. This topic details proper usage of these tags.

Section 3.1: Using Headings

Headings can be used to describe the topic they precede and they are defined with the **<h1>** to **<h6>** tags. Headings support all the global   attributes.
<h1> defines the most important heading.
<h6> defines the least important heading.
Defining a heading:

<h1> Heading 1**</h1>** **<h2>**Heading 2**</h2>**
<h3>Heading 3**</h3>** **<h4>**Heading 4**</h4>**
<h5>Heading 5**</h5>** **<h6>**Heading 6**</h6>**

Correct **structure** **matters**
Search engines and other **user agents** usually index page content based on heading elements, for example to create a table of contents, so using the correct structure for headings is

important.

In general, an article should have one h1 element for the main title followed by h2 subtitles – going down a layer if necessary. If there are h1 elements on a higher level they shoudn't be used to describe any lower level content.

Example document (extra intendation to illustrate hierarchy):

<h1>Main title**</h1>** **<p>**Introduction**</p>**
<h2>Reasons**</h2>**
<h3>Reason 1**</h3>** **<p>**Paragraph**</p>**
<h3>Reason 2**</h3>** **<p>**Paragraph**</p>**
<h2>In conclusion**</h2>** **<p>**Paragraph**</p>**

Chapter 4: Paragraphs

Column	Column
<p> Defines a paragraph
** ** Inserts a single line break
<pre> Defines pre-formatted text

Paragraphs are the most basic HTML element. This topic explains and demonstrates the usage of the paragraph element in HTML.

Section 4.1: HTML Paragraphs
The HTML **<p>** element defines a **paragraph**:
<p>This is a paragraph.**</p>**
<p>This is another paragraph.**</p>**
Display
You cannot be sure how HTML will be displayed.
Large or small screens, and resized windows will create different results.
With HTML, you cannot change the output by adding extra spaces or extra lines in your HTML code.
The browser will remove any extra spaces and extra lines when the page is displayed: **<p>**This is another paragraph, extra spaces will be removed by browsers**</p>**

Chapter 5: Text Formatting

While most HTML tags are used to create elements, HTML also provides in-text formatting tags to apply specific text-related styles to portions of text. This topic includes examples of HTML text formatting such as highlighting, bolding, underlining, subscript, and stricken text.

Section 5.1: Highlighting

The **<mark>** element is new in HTML5 and is used to mark or highlight text in a document "due to its relevance in another context".[1] The most common example would be in the results of a search were the user has entered a search query and results are shown highlighting the desired query.

<p> Here is some content from an article that contains the **<mark>**searched query**</mark>** that we are looking for. Highlighting the text will make it easier for the user to find what they are looking for.**</p>**

Output:

Here is some content from an article that contains the searched query that we are looking for. Highlighting he text will make it easier for the user to find what they are looking for.

A

common standard formatting is black text on a yellow background, but this can be changed with CSS.

Section 5.2: Bold, Italic, and Underline
Bold Text

To bold text, use the **<strong>** or **<b>** tags:
<strong>Bold   Text   Here**</strong>**
or
<b>Bold Text Here**</b>**

What 's the difference? Semantics. **<strong>** is used to indicate that the text is fundamentally or semantically *important* to the surrounding text, while **<b>** indicates no such importance and simply represents text that should be bolded.

If you were to use **<b>** a text-to-speech program would not say the word(s) any differently than any of the other words around it - you are simply drawing attention to them without adding any additional importance. By using **<strong>**, though, the same program would want to speak those word(s) with a different tone of voice to convey that the text is important in some way.

Italic   **Text**
To italicize text, use the **<em>** or **<i>** tags:
<em>Italicized   Text   Here**</em>**
or

<i>Italicized Text Here**</i>**
What's the difference? Semantics. **<em>** is used to indicate that the text should have extra emphasis that should be stressed, while **<i>** simply represents text which should be set off from the normal text around it. For example, if you wanted to stress the action inside a sentence, one might do so by emphasizing it in italics via **<em>**: "Would you just *submit* the edit already?" But if you were identifying a book or newspaper that you would normally italicize stylistically, you would simply use **<i>**: "I was forced to read *Romeo and Juliet* in high school.
Underlined Text

While the **<u>** element itself was deprecated in HTMl 4, it was reintroduced with alternate semantic meaning in HTML 5 - to represent an unarticulated, non-textual annotation. You might use such a rendering to indicate misspelled text on the page, or for a Chinese proper name mark.

<p>This paragraph contains some **<u>**mispelled**</u>** text.**</p>**

Section 5.3: Abbreviation
To mark some expression as an abbreviation, use **<abbr>** tag:
<p>I like to write **<abbr** title="Hypertext Markup Language">HTML**</abbr>**!**</p>** If

present, the title attribute is used to present the full description of such abbreviation.

Section 5.4: Inserted, Deleted, or Stricken
To mark text as inserted, use the **<ins>** tag: **<ins>**New Text**</ins>**
To mark text as deleted, use the **<del>** tag: **<del>**Deleted Text**</del>**
To strike through text, use the **<s>** tag: **<s>**Struck-through text here**</s>**

Section 5.5: Superscript and Subscript
To offset text either upward or downward you can use the tags **<sup>** and **<sub>**. To create superscript: **^{**superscript here**}**
To create subscript: **_{**subscript here**}**

Chapter 6: Anchors And Hyperlinks

Parameter   **Details**

Specifies the destination address. It can be an absolute or relative URL, or the name of an anchor. An absolute URL is the complete URL of a website like http://example.com/. A relative URL points to

href another directory and/or document inside the same website, e.g. /about-us/ points to the directory "about-us" inside the root directory (/). When pointing to another directory without explicitly specifying the document, web servers typically return the document "index.html" inside that directory.

hreflang
Specifies the language of the resource linked by the href attribute (which must be present with this one). Use language values from BCP 47 for HTML5 and RFC 1766 for HTML 4.
rel
Specifies the relationship between the current document and the linked document. For HTML5, the values must be defined in the specification or registered in the Microformats wiki.

Specifies where to open the link, e.g. in a new tab or window. Possible values are _blank, _self, target _parent, _top, and framename (deprecated). Forcing such behaviour is not recommended since it violates the control of the user over a website.

Specifies extra information about a link. The information is most often shown as a tooltip text when title the cursor moves over the link. This attribute is not restricted to links, it can be used on almost all HTML tags.

Specifies that the target will be downloaded when a user clicks on the hyperlink. The value of the download

attribute will be the name of the downloaded file. There are no restrictions on allowed values, and the browser will automatically detect the correct file extension and add it to the file (.img, .pdf, etc.). If the value is omitted, the original filename is used.

Anchor tags are commonly used to link separate webpages, but they can also be used to link between different places in a single document, often within table of contents or even launch external applications. This topic explains the implementation and application of HTML anchor tags in various roles.

Section 6.1: Link to another site

This is the basic use of the **<a>** (anchor element) element:

<a href="http://example.com/">Link to example.com**</a>**

It creates a hyperlink, to the URL http://example.com/ as specified by the href (hypertext reference) attribute, with the anchor text "Link to example.com". It would look something like the following:

Link to example.com

To denote that this link leads to an external website, you can use the external link type:

<a href="http://example.com/" rel="external">example site**</a>**

You can link to a site that uses a protocol other than HTTP. For example, to link to an FTP site, you can do,

<a href="ftp://example.com/">This could be a link to a FTP site**</a>**

In this case, the difference is that this anchor tag is requesting that the user's browser connect to example.com using the File Transfer Protocol (FTP) rather than the Hypertext Transfer Protocol (HTTP).

This could be a link to a FTP site

Section 6.2: Link to an anchor

Anchors can be used to jump to specific tags on an HTML page. The **\<a\>** tag can point to any element that has an id attribute. To learn more about IDs, visit the documentation about Classes and IDs. Anchors are mostly used to jump to a subsection of a page and are used in conjunction with header tags.

Suppose you've created a page (page1.html) on many topics:

```
<h2>                    First          topic</h2>
 <p>Content    about    the    first    topic</p>
<h2>Second                             topic</h2>
 <p>Content about the second topic</p>
```

Once you have several sections, you may want to create a Table of Contents at the top of the page with quick-links (or bookmarks) to specific sections.
If you gave an id attribute to your topics, you could then link to them

```
<h2   id="Topic1">First topic</h2>  <p>Content about the first topic</p> <h2 id="Topic2">Second topic</h2>    <p>Content about the second topic</p>
```

Now you can use the anchor in your table of contents:

<h1> Table of Contents**</h1>**
<a href='#Topic1'**>**Click to jump to the First Topic**</a> <a** href='#Topic2'**>**Click to jump to the Second Topic**</a>**

These anchors are also attached to the web page they're on (page1.html). So you can link across the site from one page to the other by referencing the page *and* anchor name. Remember, you can always **<a** href="page1.html#Topic1"**>**look back in the First Topic**</a>** for supporting information.

Section 6.3: Link to a page on the same site
You can use a relative path to link to pages on the same website.
<a href="/example"**>**Text Here**</a>**
The above example would go to the file example at the root directory (/) of the server.
If this link was on http://example.com, the following two links would bring the user to the same location
<a href="/page"**>**Text Here**</a>**
<a href="http://example.com/page"**>**Text Here**</a>**
Both of the above would go to the page file at the root directory of example.com.

Section 6.4: Link that dials a number
If the value of the href-attribute begins with tel:, your device will dial the number when you

click it. This works on mobile devices or on computers/tablets running software – like Skype or FaceTime – that can make phone calls. **<a** href="tel:11234567890">Call us**</a>** Most devices and programs will prompt the user in some way to confirm the number they are about to dial.

Section 6.5: Open link in new tab/window
<a
 href="example.com"   target="_blank">Text Here**</a>**
 The target attribute specifies where to open the link. By setting it to _blank, you tell the browser to open it in a new tab or window (per user   preference).
 SECURITY VULNERABILITY WARNING!

Using target="_blank" gives the opening site partial access to the window.opener object via JavaScript, which allows that page to then access and change the window.opener.location of *your* page and potentially redirect users to malware or phishing sites.

Whenever using this for pages you do not control, add rel="noopener" to your link to prevent the window.opener object from being sent   with   the   request.
Currently, Firefox does not support noopener,

so you will need to use rel="noopener noreferrer" for maximum effect.

Section 6.6: Link that runs JavaScript

Simply use the javascript: protocol to run the text as JavaScript instead of opening it as a normal link:

```
<a href="javascript:myFunction();">Run Code</a>
```

You can also achieve the same thing using the onclick attribute:

```
<a href="#" onclick="myFunction(); return false;">Run Code</a>
```

The return false; is necessary to prevent your page from scrolling to the top when the link to # is clicked. Make sure to include all code you'd like to run before it, as returning will stop execution of further code.

Also noteworthy, you can include an exclamation mark ! after the hashtag in order to prevent the page from scrolling to the top. This works because any invalid slug will cause the link to not scroll *anywhere* on the page, because it couldn't locate the element it references (an element with id="!"). You could also just use any invalid slug (such as #scrollsNowhere) to achieve the same effect. In this case, return false; is not required:

```
<a      href="#!"      onclick="myFunction();">Run
Code</a>
```
Should you be using any of this?

The answer is almost certainly *no*. Running
JavaScript inline with the element like this is fairly
bad practice. Consider using pure JavaScript
solutions that look for the element in the page
and bind a function to it instead. Listening for an
event

Also consider whether this element is really a
button instead of a *link*. If so, you should use
<button>.

Section 6.7: Link that runs email client
Basic usage

If the value of the href-attribute begins with
mailto: it will try to open an email client on
click:
```
<a
href="mailto:example@example.com">Send
email</a>
```
This   will   put   the   email   address
example@example.com as the recipient for the
newly   created   email.
Cc   and   Bcc
You can also add addresses for cc- or bcc-
recipients   using   the   following   syntax:
```
<a
```

href="mailto:example@example.com?cc=john @example.com&bcc=jane@example.com">Sen d   email**</a>**

Subject   and   body   text
You can populate the subject and body for the new   email   as   well:
<a
href="mailto:example@example.com?subject= Example+subject&body=Message+text"**>Send** email**</a>**
Those values must be URL encoded.

Clicking on a link with mailto: will try to open the default email client specified by your operating system or it will ask you to choose what client you want to use. Not all options specified after the recipient's address are supported in all email clients.

Chapter 7: Lists

HTML offers three ways for specifying lists: ordered lists, unordered lists, and description lists. Ordered lists use ordinal sequences to indicate the order of list elements, unordered lists use a defined symbol such as a bullet to list elements in no designated order, and description lists use indents to list elements with their children. This topic explains the implementation and combination of these lists in HTML markup.

Section 7.1: Ordered List

An ordered list can be created with the **<ol>** tag and each list item can be created with the **<li>** tag as in the example below:

```
<ol>
 <li>Item</li>
 <li>Another                    Item</li>
 <li>Yet Another Item</li>

 </ol>
```

This will produce a numbered list (which is the default style):

1.   Item
2.   Another   Item
3. Yet Another Item

Manually changing the numbers

There are a couple of ways you can play with which numbers appear on the list items in an ordered list. The first way is to set a starting number, using the start attribute. The list will start at this defined number, and continue incrementing by one as usual.

```
<ol                                    start="3">
 <li>Item</li>
 <li>Some Other Item</li> <li>Yet Another
Item</li>

 </ol>
```

This will produce a numbered list (which is the default style):

3.   Item
4.   Some   Other   Item
5. Yet Another Item

You can also explicitly set a certain list item to a specific number. Further list items after one with a specified value will continue incrementing by one from that list item's value, ignoring where the parent list was at.
`<li value="7"></li>`

It is also worth noting that, by using the value attribute directly on a list item, you can override an ordered list's existing numbering system by restarting the numbering at a lower value. So if the parent list was already up to value 7, and encountered a list item at value 4, then that list item would still display as 4 and continue counting from that point again.

```
<ol                                   start="5">
 <li>Item</li>
 <li>Some            Other            Item</li>
 <li value="4">A   Reset   Item</li>  <li>Another
Item</li>
 <li>Yet Another Item</li>

</ol>
```

So the example above will produce a list that follows the numbering pattern of 5, 6, 4, 5, 6 - starting again at a number lower than the previous and duplicating the number 6 in the list.

Note: The start and value attributes only accept a number - even if the ordered list is set to display as Roman numerals or letters.

You can reverse the numbering by adding reversed in your ol element:

```
<ol                                  reversed>
 <li>Item</li>
 <li>Some            Other            Item</li>
 <li value="4">A   Reset   Item</li>  <li>Another
Item</li>
 <li>Yet Another Item</li>
```

</ol>

Reverse numbering is helpful if you're continually adding to a list, such as with new podcast episodes or presentations, and you want the most recent items to appear first.

Changing the type of numeral

You can easily change the type of numeral shown in the list item marker by using the type attribute

<ol   type="1|a|A|i|I">

Type Description Examples 1Default value - Decimal numbers 1,2,3,4 aAlphabetically ordered (lowercase) a,b,c,d AAlphabetically ordered (uppercase) A,B,C,D

iRoman Numerals (lowercase)

I Roman Numerals (uppercase) i,ii,iii,iv I,II,III,IV

You should use ol to display a list of items, where the items have been intentionally ordered and order should be emphasized. If changing the order of the items does NOT make the list incorrect, you should use **<ul>**.

Section 7.2: Unordered List

An unordered list can be created with the **<ul>** tag and each list item can be created with the **<li>** tag as shown by the example below:

29

```html
<ul>
<li>Item</li>
<li>Another Item</li> <li>Yet Another Item</li>

</ul>
```

This will produce a bulleted list (which is the default style):

Item

Another   Item

Yet Another Item

You should use ul to display a list of items, where the order of the items is not important. If changing the order of the items makes the list incorrect, you should use **<ol>**.

Section 7.3: Nested lists
You can nest lists to represent sub-items of a list item.

```html
<ul>
<li>item                                            1</li>
<li>item 2

<ul>
<li>sub-item                                      2.1</li>
<li>sub-item 2.2</li>

</ul>
</li>
<li>item 3</li>
```

```
</ul>
```

item 1 item 2 sub-item 2.1 sub-item 2.2 item 3

The nested list has to be a child of the li element.
You can nest different types of list, too:

```
<ol> <li>Hello, list!</li> <li>
```

```
<ul>        <li>Hello,        nested        list!</li>
</ul>
</li>
</ol>
```

Section 7.4: Description List
A description list (or *definition list*, as it was called before HTML5) can be created with the dl element. It consists of name-value groups, where the name is given in the dt element, and the value is given in the dd element.

```
<dl>
<dt>name                                    1</dt>
<dd>value    for    1</dd>    <dt>name    2</dt>
<dd>value for 2</dd>
```

```
</dl>
```
Live   demo
A name-value group can have more than one

31

name and/or more than one value (which represent alternatives):

```
<dl>

<dt>                    name                    1</dt>
<dt>name                                        2</dt>
<dd>value for 1 and 2</dd>

<dt>                    name                    3</dt>
<dd>value for 3</dd> <dd>value for 3</dd>

</dl>
```

Live demo

Chapter 8: Tables

The HTML **<table>** element allows web authors to display tabular data (such as text, images, links, other tables, etc.) in a two dimensional table with rows and columns of cells.

Section 8.1: Simple Table

```
<table>
 <tr>
 <th>Heading           1/Column          1</th>
 <th>Heading 2/Column 2</th>

 </tr>
 <tr>
 <td>Row     1     Data     Column     1</td>
 <td>Row     1     Data     Column     2</td>
 </tr>
 <tr>
 <td>Row     2     Data     Column     1</td>
 <td>Row     2     Data     Column     2</td>
 </tr>
 </table>
```

This will render a **<table>** consisting of three total rows (**<tr>**): one row of header cells (**<th>**) and two rows of content cells (**<td>**). **<th>** elements are *tabular headers* and **<td>** elements are *tabular data*. You can put whatever you want inside a **<td>** or **<th>**.

Heading 1/Column 1 Heading 2/Column 2 Row 1 Data Column 1 Row 1 Data Column 2 Row 2 Data Column 1 Row 2 Data Column 2

Section 8.2: Spanning columns or rows
Table cells can span multiple columns or rows using the colspan and rowspan attributes. These attributes can be applied to **<th>** and **<td>** elements.

```
<table>
 <tr>
 <td>row 1 col 1</td> <td>row 1 col 2</td> <td>row 1 col 3</td>

 </tr>
  <tr>

<td colspan="3">This second row spans all three columns</td>                    </tr>
 <tr>

<td rowspan="2">This cell spans two rows</td> <td>row        3        col        2</td> <td>row 3 col 3</td>

</tr>
 <tr>
 <td>row 4 col 2</td> <td>row 4 col 3</td> </tr>
```

</table>

Will   result   in

row 1 col 1	row 1 col 2	row 1 col 3
This second row spans all three columns		
This cell spans two rows	row 3 col 2	row 3 col 3
	row 4 col 2	row 4 col 3

Note that you should not design a table where both rows and columns overlap as this is invalid HTML and the result is handled differently by different web browsers.

rowspan = A non-negative integer that specifies the number of rows spanned by a cell. The default value of this attribute is one (1). A value of zero (0) means that the cell will extend from the current row until the last row of the table (**<thead>**, **<tbody>**, or **<tfoot>**).

colspan = A non-negative integer that specifies the number of columns spanned by the current cell. The default value of this attribute is one (1). A value of zero (0) means that the cell will extend from the current to the last column of the column group **<colgroup>** in which the cell is defined.

Section 8.3: Column Groups

35

Sometimes you may want to apply styling to a column or group of columns. Or for semantic purposes, you may want to group columns together. To do this, use **<colgroup>** and **<col>** elements.

The optional **<colgroup>** tag allows you to group columns together. **<colgroup>** elements must be child elements of a **<table>** and must come after any **<caption>** elements and before any table content (e.g., **<tr>**, **<thead>**, **<tbody>**, etc.).

```
<table>
 <colgroup              span="2"></colgroup>
 <colgroup              span="2"></colgroup>
 ...

</table>
```

The optional **<col>** tag allows you to reference individual columns or a range of columns without applying a logical grouping. **<col>** elements are optional, but if present, they must be inside a **<colgroup>** element.

```
<table>
 <colgroup>
 <col         id="MySpecialColumn"              />
 <col />

</colgroup>
 <colgroup>
```

```
<col           class="CoolColumn"                />
<col     class="NeatColumn"     span="2"     />
</colgroup>
```

...

```
</table>
```

The following CSS styles can be applied to **<colgroup>** and **<col>** elements:
border
background   width
visibility
display   (as   in   display: none)
display: none; will actually remove the columns from the display, causing the table to render as if   those   cells   don't   exist
For more information, see HTML5 Tabular data.

Section 8.4: Table with thead, tbody, tfoot, and caption
HTML also provides the tables with the **<thead>**, **<tbody>**, **<tfoot>**, and **<caption>** elements. These additional elements are useful for adding semantic value to your tables and for providing a place for separate CSS styling. When printing out a table that doesn't fit onto one (paper) page, most browsers repeat the contents of **<thead>** on every page. There's a specific order that must be adhered to, and we should be aware that not every element falls into place as one would expect.

The following example demonstrates how our 4 elements should be placed.
<table>
<caption>Table Title**</caption>** <!--| caption is the first child of table |->

<thead> <!--=====================| thead is after caption |->
<tr>
<th>Header content 1**</th>**
<th>Header content 2**</th>**

</tr>
</thead>

<tbody> <!--=====================| tbody is after thead |-> **<tr>**
<td>Body content 1**</td>**
<td>Body content 2**</td>**

</tr>
</tbody>
<tfoot><!--| tfoot can be placed before or after tbody, but not in a group of tbody. |-> <!--| Regardless where tfoot is in markup, it is rendered at the bottom. |->

<tr>
<td>Footer content 1**</td>** **<td>**Footer content 2**</td>**

38

```
    </tr>
   </tfoot>
  </table>
```

The following example's results are demonstrated twice--the first table lacks any styles, the second table has a few CSS properties applied: background-color, color, and border*. The styles are provided as a visual guide and is not an essential aspect of the topic at hand.

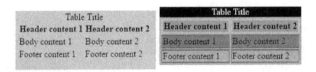

Element	Styles	Applies
<caption>	Yellow text on black	background.
<thead>	Bold text on purple	background.
<tbody>	Text on blue	background.
<tfoot>	Text on green	background.
<th>	Orange	borders.
<td>	Red borders.	

Section 8.5: Heading scope

th elements are very commonly used to indicate headings for table rows and columns, like   so:

```
  <table>
   <thead>
```

```
<tr>
<td></td>
<th>Column    Heading    1</th>    <th>Column
Heading 2</th>

</tr>
</thead>
<tbody>

<tr>
<th>Row    Heading    1</th>    <td></td>
<td></td>

</tr>
<tr>
<th>Row    Heading    2</th>    <td></td>
<td></td>
</tr>
</tbody>
</table>
```

This can be improved for accessibility by the
use of the scope attribute. The above example
would   be   amended   as   follows:

```
<table>
<thead>

<tr>                                    <td></td>
<th scope="col">Column Heading 1</th> <th
scope="col">Column Heading 2</th>

</tr> </thead> <tbody>
```

```html
<tr>   <th   scope="row">Row   Heading   1</th>
<td></td>
 <td></td>

</tr>
 <tr>
 <th      scope="row">Row      Heading      1</th>
<td></td>
 <td></td>
 </tr>
 </tbody>
 </table>
```

scope is known as an *enumerated attribute,* meaning that it can have a value from a specific set of possible values. This set includes:

col
 row
 colgroup rowgroup

References:

https://developer.mozilla.org/en-US/docs/Web/HTML/Element/th#attr-scope
https://www.w3.org/TR/WCAG20-TECHS/H63.html

Chapter 9: Comments

Similar to other programming, markup, and markdown languages, comments in HTML provide other developers with development specific information without affecting the user interface. Unlike other languages however, HTML comments can be used to specify HTML elements for Internet Explorer only. This topic explains how to write HTML comments, and their functional applications.

Section 9.1: Creating comments

HTML comments can be used to leave notes to yourself or other developers about a specific point in code. They can be initiated with <!- and concluded with -->, like so:

```
<!-- I'm an HTML comment! -->
```

They can be incorporated inline within other content:

<h1>This part will be displayed <!-- while this will not be displayed ->.**</h1>**

They can also span multiple lines to provide more information:

<!-- This is a multiline HTML comment. Whatever is in here will not be rendered by the browser.

You can "comment out" entire sections of HTML code.

    ->
    However, they **cannot** appear within another HTML tag, like this:
    <h1 <!-- testAttribute="something" ->>This will not work**</h1>**

This produces invalid HTML as the entire **<h1** <!-- testAttribute="something" -> block would be considered a single start tag h1 with some other invalid information contained within it, followed by a single > closing bracket that does nothing.

    For compatibility with tools that try to parse HTML as XML or SGML, the body of your comment should not contain two dashes -.

    Section 9.2: Commenting out whitespace between inline elements

Inline display elements, usually such as span or a, will include up to one white-space character before and after them in the document. In order to avoid very long lines in the markup (that are hard to read) and unintentional white-space (which affects formatting), the white-space can be commented out.

```html
<!-- Use an HTML comment to nullify the newline
character                        below:                 -->
<a href="#">I hope there will be no extra
whitespace               after          this!</a><!-
--><button>Foo</button>
```

Try it without a comment between the inline
elements, and there will be one space between
them. Sometimes picking up the space
character   is   desired.
Example code:

```html
<!-- Use an HTML comment to nullify the newline
character              below:                  ->
<a href="#">I hope there will be no extra
whitespace               after          this!</a><!-
-><button>Foo</button>
<hr>
<!-- Without it, you can notice a small formatting
difference: -> <a href="#">I hope there will be no
extra      whitespace      after      this!</a>
<button>Foo</button>
```

Output:

I hope there will be no extra whitespace after this! Foo
I hope there will be no extra whitespace after this! Foo

44

Chapter 10: Classes And Ids

Parameter	Details
class	Indicates the Class of the element (non-unique)
id	Indicates the ID of the element (unique in the same context)

Classes and IDs make referencing HTML elements from scripts and stylesheets easier. The class attribute can be used on one or more tags and is used by CSS for styling. IDs however are intended to refer to a single element, meaning the same ID should never be used twice. IDs are generally used with JavaScript and internal document links, and are discouraged in CSS. This topic contains helpful explanations and examples regarding proper usage of class and ID attributes in HTML.

Section 10.1: Giving an element a class

Classes are identifiers for the elements that they are assigned to. Use the class attribute to assign a class to an element.

<div class="example-class"**></div>**

To assign multiple classes to an element, separate the class names with spaces.

<div class="class1 class2"**></div>**

Using classes in CSS

Classes can be used for styling certain elements without changing all elements of that kind. For example, these two span elements can have completely different stylings:

```
<span></span>
<span                    class="special"></span>
```

Classes of the same name can be given to any number of elements on a page and they will all receive the styling associated with that class. This will always be true unless you specify the element within the CSS.
For example, we have two elements, both with the class highlight:

```
<div class="highlight">Lorem ipsum</div>
<span class="highlight">Lorem ipsum</span>
```

If our CSS is as below, then the color green will be applied to the text within both elements:

```
.highlight    {    color:    green;    }
```

However, if we only want to target div's with the class highlight then we can add specificity like below:

```
div.highlight    {    color:    green;    }
```

Nevertheless, when styling with CSS, it is generally recommended that only classes (e.g. .highlight) be used rather than elements with classes (e.g. div.highlight).
As with any other selector, classes can can be nested:

```
.main .highlight { color: red; } /* Descendant combinator                              */
.footer > .highlight { color: blue; } /* Child combinator                              */
```

You can also chain the class selector to only

select elements that have a combination of several classes. For example, if this is our HTML:
<div class="special left menu"**>**This text will be pink**</div>**
And we want to colour this specific piece of text pink, we can do the following in our CSS:
.special.left.menu { color: pink; }

Section 10.2: Giving an element an ID
The ID attribute of an element is an identifier which must be unique in the whole document. Its purpose is to uniquely identify the element when linking (using an anchor), scripting, or styling (with CSS).
<div id="example-id"**></div>**
You should not have two elements with the same ID in the same document, even if the attributes are attached to two different kinds of elements. For example, the following code is incorrect:
<div id="example-id"**></div>** **<span** id="example-id"**></span>**
Browsers will do their best to render this code, but unexpected behavior may occur when styling with CSS or adding functionality with JavaScript.
To reference elements by their ID in CSS, prefix the ID with #.
#exampleid { color: green; }
To jump to an element with an ID on a given page, append # with the element name in the

URL.

http://example.com/about#exampleid   This feature is supported in most browsers and does not require additional JavaScript or CSS to work.

Section 10.3: Acceptable Values
For an ID

Version   ≥   5

The only restrictions on the value of an id are:

1. it must be unique in the document
2. it must not contain any space characters
3. it must contain at least one character

So the value can be all digits, just one digit, just punctuation characters, include special characters, whatever. Just no whitespace. So these are valid:

<div id="container"**>** ... **</div>**
<div id="999"**>** ... **</div> <div** id="#%LV-||"**>** ... **</div> <div** id="____V"**>** ... **</div> <div** id="⌘⌐"**>** ... **</div> <div** id="♥"**>** ... **</div>**
<div id="{}"**>** ... **</div> <div** id="©"**>** ... **</div>**
<div id="⇧₩¤☆€~¥"**>** ... **</div>**

This   is   invalid:
<div id="   "**>** ... **</div>**
This is also invalid, when included in the same document:

48

<div id="results"**>** ... **</div> <div** id="results"**>** ... **</div>** Version ≤ 4.01

An id value must begin with a letter, which can then be followed only by:

letters (A-Z/a-z) digits (0-9)
hyphens ("-")
underscores ("_") colons (":")
periods (".")

Referring to the first group of examples in the HTML5 section above, only one is valid: **<div** id="container"**>** ... **</div>** These are also valid:

<div id="sampletext"**>** ... **</div> <div** id="sample-text"**>** ... **</div> <div** id="sample_text"**>** ... **</div> <div** id="sample:text"**>** ... **</div> <div** id="sample.text"**>** ... **</div>**

Again, if it doesn't start with a letter (uppercase or lowercase), it's not valid.
For a Class
The rules for classes are essentially the same as for an id. The difference is that class values *do not* need to be unique in the document. Referring to the examples above, although this is not valid in the same document: **<div** id="results"**>** ... **</div> <div** id="results"**>** ... **</div>** This is perfectly okay:

49

```
<div   class="results">   ...   </div>   <div
class="results">                ...                </div>
```

Important Note: How ID and Class values are treated outside of HTML

Keep in mind that the rules and examples above apply within the context of HTML. Using numbers, punctuation or special characters in the value of an id or a class may cause trouble in other contexts, such as CSS, JavaScript and regular expressions. For example, although the following id is valid in   HTML5:

```
<div          id="9lions">          ...          </div>
```

...   it   is   invalid   in   CSS:

4.1.3 Characters and case

In CSS, *identifiers* (including element names, classes, and IDs in selectors) can contain only the characters [a-zA-Z0-9] and ISO 10646 characters U+00A0 and higher, plus the hyphen (-) and the underscore (_); *they cannot start with a digit, two hyphens, or a hyphen followed by a digit*. (emphasis added)

In most cases you may be able to escape characters in contexts where they have restrictions or special meaning.

W3C References

Section 10.4: Problems related to duplicated IDs
Having more than one element with the same ID is a hard to troubleshoot problem. The HTML parser will usually try to render the page in any case. Usually no error occurs. But the pace could end up in a mis-behaving web page. In   this   example:

```
<div                  id="aDiv">a</div>
<div                  id="aDiv">b</div>
```

CSS selectors still work

```
#aDiv                                        {
color:                                    red;
}
```

But JavaScript fails to handle both elements:

```
var                  html                  =
document.getElementById("aDiv").innerHTML;
```

In this casehtml variable bears only the first div content ("a").

Chapter 11: Data Attributes

Value Description

somevalue Specifies the value of the attribute (as a string)

Section 11.1: Older browsers support
Data attributes were introduced in HTML5 which is supported by all modern browsers, but older browsers before HTML5 don't recognize the data attributes. However, in HTML specifications, attributes that are not recognized by the browser must be left alone and the browser will simply ignore them when rendering the page.

Web developers have utilized this fact to create non-standard attributes which are any attributes not part of the HTML specifications. For example, the value attribute in the line bellow is considered a non-standard attribute because the specifications for the **<img>** tag don't have a value attribute and it is not a global attribute:

<img src="sample.jpg" value="test" **/>**

This means that although data attributes are not supported in older browsers, they still work and you can set and retrieve them using the same generic JavaScript setAttribute and getAttribute

52

methods, but you cannot use the new dataset property which is only supported in modern browsers.

Section 11.2: Data Attribute Use
HTML5 data-* attributes provide a convenient way to store data in HTML elements. The stored data can be read or modified using JavaScript

```
<div data-submitted="yes" class="user_profile">
...          some          content          ...
</div>
```

Data attribute structure is data-*, i.e. the name of the data attribute comes after the data part. Using this name, the attribute can be accessed. Data in string format (including json) can be stored using data-* attribute.

Chapter 12: Linking Resources

Attribute	Details
charset	Specifies the character encoding of the linked document
crossorigin	Specifies how the element handles cross origin requests
href	Specifies the location of the linked document
hreflang	Specifies the language of the text in the linked document
media	Specifies on what device the linked document will be displayed, often used with selecting stylesheets based on the device in question
rel	**Required**. Specifies the relationship between the current document and the linked document
rev	Specifies the relationship between the linked document and the current document
sizes	Specifies the size of the linked resource. Only when rel="icon"
target	Specifies where the linked document is to be loaded
type	Specifies the media type of the linked document
integrity	Specifies a base64 encoded hash (sha256, sha384, or sha512) of the linked resource allowing the browser to verify its legitimacy.

While many scripts, icons, and stylesheets can be written straight into HTML markup, it is best practice and more efficient to include these resources in their own file and link them to your document. This topic covers linking external resources such as stylesheets and scripts into an HTML document.

Section 12.1: JavaScript

Synchronous

<script src="path/to.js"**></script>**

Standard practice is to place JavaScript **<script>** tags just before the closing **</body>** tag. Loading your scripts last allows your site's visuals to show up more quickly and discourages your JavaScript from trying to interact with elements that haven't loaded yet.

Asynchronous

<script src="path/to.js" async**></script>**

Another alternative, when the Javascript code being loaded is not necessary for page initialization, it can be loaded asynchronously, speeding up the page load. Using async the browser will load the contents of the script in parallel and, once it is fully downloaded, will interrupt the HTML parsing in order to parse the Javascript file.

Deferred

<script src="path/to.js" defer**></script>**

Deferred scripts are like async scripts, with the exception that the parsing will only be performed once the HTML is fully parsed. Deferred scripts are guaranteed to be loaded in the order of declaration, same way as synchronous scripts.

<noscript>

<noscript>JavaScript   disabled**</noscript>**
The **<noscript>** element defines content to be displayed if the user has scripts disabled or if the browser does not support using scripts. The **<noscript>** tag can be placed in either the **<head>** or the **<body>**.

Section 12.2: External CSS Stylesheet

<link
rel="stylesheet"   href="path/to.css"
type="text/css"**>**

The standard practice is to place CSS **<link>** tags inside the **<head>** tag at the top of your HTML. This way the CSS will be loaded first and will apply to your page as it is loading, rather than showing unstyled HTML until the CSS is loaded. The typeattribute is not necessary in HTML5, because HTML5 usually supports CSS.

```html
<link rel="stylesheet" href="path/to.css" type="text/css">
```
and
```html
<link rel="stylesheet" href="path/to.css">
```
... do the same thing in HTML5. Another, though less common practice, is to use an @import statement inside direct CSS. Like this:

```html
<style type="text/css">
@import("path/to.css")
</style>
```

```html
<style>
@import("path/to.css")
</style>
```

Section 12.3: Favicon
```html
<link rel="icon" type="image/png" href="/favicon.png">
<link rel="shortcut icon" type="image/x-icon" href="/favicon.ico">
```
Use the mime-type image/png for PNG files and image/x-icon for icon (*.ico) files. For the difference, see this SO question. A file named favicon.ico at the root of your website will typically be loaded and applied automatically, without the need for a `<link>`

tag. If this file ever changes, browsers can be slow and stubborn about updating their cache.

Section 12.4: Alternative CSS

```
<link
 rel="alternate                    stylesheet"
 href="path/to/style.css"       title="yourTitle">
```

Some browsers allow alternate style sheets to apply if they are offered. By default they will not be applied, but usually they can be changed through the browser settings:

Firefox lets the user select the stylesheet using the View > Page Style submenu, Internet Explorer also supports this feature (beginning with IE 8), also accessed from View > Page Style (at least as of IE 11), but Chrome requires an extension to use the feature (as of version 48). The web page can also provide its own user interface to let the user switch styles.

(Source: the MDN Docs)

Section 12.5: Resource Hint: dns-prefetch, prefetch, prerender

Preconnect

The preconnect relationship is similar to dns-prefetch in that it will resolve the DNS. However, it will also make the TCP handshake, and optional TLS negotiation. This is an

experimental   feature.
<link   rel="preconnect"   href="URL"**>**

DNS-Prefetch

Informs browsers to resolve the DNS for a URL, so that all assets from that URL load faster.

<link   rel="dns-prefetch"   href="URL"**>**

Prefetch

Informs the browsers that a given resource should be prefetched so it can be loaded more quickly.

<link   rel="prefetch"   href="URL"**>**

DNS-Prefetch resolves only the domain name whereas prefetch downloads/stores the specified   resources.

Prerender

Informs browsers to fetch and render the URL in the background, so that they can be delivered to the user instantaneously as the user navigates to that URL. This is an experimental   feature.

<link rel="prerender" href="URL"**>**

Section 12.6: Link 'media' attribute

<link
rel="stylesheet" href="test.css" media="print"**>**
Media specifies what style sheet should be used for what type of media. Using the print value would only display that style sheet for print   pages.
The value of this attribute can be any of the

mediatype values (similar to a CSS media query).

Section 12.7: Prev and Next

When a page is part of a series of articles, for instance, one can use prev and next to point to pages that are coming before and after.

```
<link                              rel="prev"
href="http://stackoverflow.com/documentatio
n/java/topics">
<link                              rel="next"
href="http://stackoverflow.com/documentatio
n/css/topics">
```

Section 12.8: Web Feed

Use the rel="alternate" attribute to allow discoverability of your Atom/RSS feeds.

```
<link                         rel="alternate"
type="application/atom+xml"
href="http://example.com/feed.xml" /> <link
rel="alternate"       type="application/rss+xml"
href="http://example.com/feed.xml" />
```
See the MDN docs for RSS feeds and Atomic RSS.

Chapter 13: Include Javascript Code In Html

Attribute   src
 type

  async
  defer
  charset

Details
Specifies the path to a JavaScript file. Either a relative or absolute URL.
Specifies the MIME type. This attribute is required in HTML4, but optional in HTML5.
Specifies that the script shall be executed asynchronously (only for external scripts). This attribute does not require any value (except of XHTML).
Specifies that the script shall be executed when the page has finished parsing (only for external scripts). This attribute does not require any value (except of XHTML).
Specifies the character encoding used in an external script file, e.g. UTF-8

  crossoriginHow the element handles crossorigin requests
  nonce Cryptographic nonce used in *Content Security Policy* checks
CSP3

61

Section 13.1: Handling disabled Javascript

It is possible that the client browser does not support Javascript or have Javascript execution disabled, perhaps due to security reasons. To be able to tell users that a script is supposed to execute in the page, the **<noscript>** tag can be used. The content of **<noscript>** is displayed whenever Javascript is disabled for the current page.

<script>
document.write("Hello,   world!");
</script>
<noscript>This browser does not support Javascript.**</noscript>**

Section 13.2: Linking to an external JavaScript file

<script
src="example.js"**></script>**

The src attribute works like the href attribute on anchors: you can either specify an absolute or relative URL. The example above links to a file inside the same directory of the HTML document. This is typically added inside the **<head>** tags at the top of the html document

Section 13.3: Directly including JavaScript code
Instead of linking to an external file, you can also include the JS code as-is in your HTML:

```
<script>
// 				JavaScript 				code
</script>
```

Section 13.4: Including a JavaScript file executing asynchronously

```
<script
 type="text/javascript" 				src="URL"
 async></script>
```

Chapter 14: Using Html With Css

CSS provides styles to HTML elements on the page. Inline styling involves usage of the style attribute in tags, and is highly discouraged. Internal stylesheets use the **<style>** tag and are used to declare rules for directed portions of the page. External stylesheets may be used through a **<link>** tag which takes an external file of CSS and applies the rules to the document. This topic covers usage of all three methods of attachment.

Section 14.1: External Stylesheet Use
Use the link attribute in the document's head:

```
<head>
 <link       rel="stylesheet"       type="text/css"
href="stylesheet.css">
 </head>
```

You can also use stylesheets provided from websites via a content delivery network, or CDN for short. (for example, Bootstrap):

```
<head>
 <link                         rel="stylesheet"

href="https://maxcdn.bootstrapcdn.com/bootstr
ap/3.3.7/css/bootstrap.min.css"        integrity==
```

BVYiiSIFeK1dGmJRAkycuHAHRg32OmUcww7on3
RYdg4Va+PmSTsz/K68vbdEjh4u"
crossorigin="anonymous">
</head>

Generally, you can find CDN support for a framework on its website.

Section 14.2: Internal Stylesheet
You can also include CSS elements internally by using the **<style>** tag:
<head>
<style type="text/css">
body {
background-color: gray;
}
</style>
</head>
Multiple internal stylesheets can be included in a program as well.
<head>
<style type="text/css">
body {
background-color: gray; }
</style>
<style type="text/css"> p {
background-color: blue; }
</style>
</head>

Section 14.3: Inline Style

You can style a specific element by using the style attribute:

```
<span style="color: red">This text will appear in red.</span>
```

Note: Try to avoid this -- the point of CSS is to separate content from presentation.

Section 14.4: Multiple Stylesheets

It's possible to load multiple stylesheets:

```
<head>
<link rel="stylesheet" type="text/css" href="general.css"> <link rel="stylesheet" type="text/css" href="specific.css">

</head>
```

Note that **later files and declarations will override earlier ones**. So if general.css contains:

```
body {
backgroundcolor: red;
}
```

and specific.css contains:

```
body {
backgroundcolor: blue;
}
```

if both are used, the background of the document will be blue.

Chapter 15: Images

Parameters	Details
src	Specifies the URL of the image
srcset	Images to use in different situations (e.g., high-resolution displays, small monitors, etc)
sizes	Image sizes between breakpoints
crossorigin	How the element handles crossorigin requests
usemap	Name of image map to use
ismap	Whether the image is a server-side image map
alt	Alternative text that should be displayed if for some reason the image could not be displayed
width	Specifies the width of the image (optional)
height	Specifies the height of the image (optional)

Section 15.1: Creating an image

To add an image to a page, use the image tag. Image tags (img) do not have closing tags. The two main attributes you give to the img tag are src, the image source and alt, which is alternative text describing the image.

```
<img src="images/hello.png" alt="Hello World">
```

You can also get images from a web URL:

```
<img src="https://i.stack.imgur.com/ALgZi.jpg?s=48&g=1" alt="StackOverflow user Caleb Kleveter">
```

Note: Images are not technically inserted into an HTML page, images are linked to HTML pages. The **<img>** tag creates a holding space for the referenced image. It is also possible to embed images directly inside the page using base64: **<img** src="data:image/png;base64,iVBOR..." alt="Hello World"**>**

Tip: To link an image to another document, simply nest the **<img>** tag inside **<a>** tags.

Section 15.2: Choosing alt text

Alt-text is used by screen readers for visually impaired users and by search engines. It's therefore important to write good alt-text for your images.

The text should look correct even if you replace the image with its alt attribute. For example:

<!-- Incorrect ->
<img src="anonymous.png" alt="Anonymous user avatar"**/>** An anonymous user wrote: **<blockquote>**Lorem ipsum dolor sed.**</blockquote>**

<a href="https://google.com/"**><img** src="edit.png" alt="Edit icon"**/></a>** /
<a href="https://google.com/"**><img** src="delete.png" alt="Delete icon"**/></a>**

Without the images, this would look like: Anonymous user avatar An anonymous user

69

wrote: Lorem ipsum dolor sed.
Edit icon / Delete icon

To correct this:

Remove the alt-text for the avatar. This image adds information for sighted users (an easily identifiable icon to show that the user is anonymous) but this information is already available in the text.1 Remove the "icon" from the alt-text for the icons. Knowing that this would be an icon if it were there does not help to convey its actual purpose.

```
<!--                    Correct                    ->
<img   src="anonymous.png"   alt=""/>   An
anonymous   user   wrote:   <blockquote>Lorem
ipsum        dolor        sed.</blockquote>
<a          href="https://google.com/"><img
src="edit.png"      alt="Edit"/></a>      /      <a
href="https://google.com/"><img
src="delete.png" alt="Delete"/></a>
```

An anonymous user wrote: Lorem ipsum dolor sed.
Edit / Delete

Footnotes

1 There is a semantic difference between including an empty alt attribute and excluding it altogether. An empty alt attribute indicates that the image is *not* a key part of the content (as is

true in this case - it's just an additive image that is not necessary to understand the rest) and thus may be omitted from rendering. However, the lack of an alt attribute indicates that the image *is* a key part of the content and that there simply is no textual equivalent available for rendering.

Section 15.3: Responsive image using the srcset attribute

Using srcset with sizes

```
<img      sizes="(min-width:  1200px)  580px,
(min-width:             640px)         48vw,
98vw"

srcset           ="img/hello-300.jpg        300w,
img/hello-600.jpg                           600w,
img/hello-900.jpg                           900w,
img/hello-1200.jpg 1200w"

src="img/hello-900.jpg"                alt="hello">
```

sizes are like media queries, describing how much space the image takes of the viewport.

if viewport is larger than 1200px, image is exactly 580px (for example our content is centered in container which is max 1200px wide. Image takes half of it minus margins).
if viewport is between 640px and 1200px, image takes 48% of viewport (for example image scales with our page and takes half of viewport width

71

minus   margins).
if viewport is any other size , in our case less than 640px, image takes 98% of viewport (for example image scales with our page and takes full width of viewport minus margins). **Media condition must be omitted for last item.**

srcset is just telling the browser what images we have available, and what are their sizes.

img /hello300.jpg is 300px wide, img/hello600.jpg is 600px wide, img/hello900.jpg is 900px wide, img/hello1200.jpg is 1200px wide

src is always mandatory image source. In case of using with srcset, src will serve fallback image in case browser is not supporting srcset.
Using srcset without sizes

<img   src="img/hello-300.jpg"   alt="hello" srcset="img/hello-300.jpg 1x, img/hello-600.jpg 2x,
 img/hello-1200.jpg 3x"**>**

srcset provides list of available images, with device-pixel ratio x descriptor.

if device-pixel ratio is 1, use img/hello300.jpg if device-pixel ratio is 2, use img/hello600.jpg if device-pixel ratio is 3, use img/hello1200.jpg src is always mandatory image source. In case of using with srcset, src will serve fallback image in case browser is not supporting srcset.

Section 15.4: Responsive image using picture element
Code

```
<picture>
  <source media="(min-width: 600px)" srcset="large_image.jpg">
  <source media="(min-width: 450px)" srcset="small_image.jpg">
  <img src="default_image.jpg" style="width:auto;">
</picture>
```

Usage

To display different images under different screen width, you must include all images using the source tag in a picture tag as shown in the above example.

Result

On screens with screen width >600px, it shows large_image.jpg On screens with screen width >450px, it shows small_image.jpg On screens with other screen width, it shows default_image.jpg

Chapter 16: Image Maps

Tag/Attribute	Value

<img>

Below are the image map-specific attributes to use with **<img>**. Regular **<img>** attributes apply.

usemap

The name of the map with a hash symbol prepended to it. For example, for a map with name="map", the image should have usemap="#map".

<map>

name The name of the map to identify it. To be used with the image's usemap attribute.

<area>

Below are **<area>**-specific attributes. When href is specified, making the **<area>** a link, **<area>** also supports all of the attributes of the anchor tag (**<a>**) except ping. See them at the MDN docs. The alternate text to display if images are not supported. This is only necessary if href is also set on alt the **<area>**.

The coordinates outlining the selectable area. When shape="polygon", this should be set to a list of coords

"x, y" pairs separated by commas (i.e., shape="polygon" coords="x1, y1, x2, y2, x3, y3, ..."). When shape="rectangle", this should be set to left, top, right, bottom. When shape="circle", this should be set to centerX, centerY, radius.

href The URL of the hyperlink, if specified. If it is omitted, then the **<area>** will not represent a hyperlink.

The shape of the **<area>**. Can be set to default to select the entire image (no coords attribute shape necessary), circle or circ for a circle, rectangle or rect for a rectangle, and polygon or poly for a polygonal area specified by corner points.

Section 16.1: Introduction to Image Maps
Description

An image maps is an image with clickable areas that usually act as hyperlinks. The image is defined by the **<img>** tag, and the map is defined by a **<map>** tag with **<area>** tags to denote each clickable area. Use the usemap and name attributes to bind the image and the map.

Basic   **Example**
To create an image map so that each of the shapes in the image below are clickable:

75

The code would be as follows:

```
<img src="http://jaced.com/blogpix/2007/trisquarecircle/002.gif" usemap="#shapes"> <map name="shapes">
 <area shape="polygon" coords="79,6,5,134,153,134">
 <area shape="rectangle" coords="177,6,306,134">
 <area shape="circle" coords="397,71,65">

</map>
```

You should see that the browser recognizes the areas when the cursor becomes a pointer. See a live demo on JSFiddle

Chapter 17: Input Control Elements

Parameter   class
  id

  type
  name
  disabled
  checked
  multiple

Details
Indicates the Class of the input
Indicates the ID of the input
Identifies the type of input control to display. Acceptable values are hidden, text, tel, url, email, password, date, time, number, range, color, checkbox, radio, file, submit, image, reset, and button. Defaults to text if not specified, if the value is invalid, or if the browser does not support the type specified.
Indicates the name of the input
Boolean value that indicates the input should be disabled. Disabled controls cannot be edited, are not sent on form submission, and cannot receive focus.
When the value of the type attribute is radio or checkbox, the presence of this Boolean attribute indicates that the control is selected by default; otherwise it is ignored.

HTML5 Indicates multiple files or values can be passed (Applies only to file and email type inputs)

placeholder
HTML5 A hint to the user of what can be entered in the control . The placeholder text must not contain carriage returns or line-feeds autocomplete**HTML5** Indicates whether the value of the control can be automatically completed by the browser.

Boolean value that indicates the input is not editable. Readonly controls are still sent on form readonly submission, but will not receive focus. **HTML5:** This attribute is ignored when the value of type attribute is either set to hidden, range, color, checkbox, radio, file or button.

required
HTML5 Indicates a value must be present or the element must be checked in order for the form to be submitted

alt
autofocus
value

step
An alternative text for images, in case they are not displayed.

The **<input>** element should get the focus when page   loads.
Specifies the value of **<input>** element.

The step attribute specifies the legal number intervals. It works with the following input types: number, range, date, datetime-local, month, time and week.

A key component of interactive web systems, input tags are HTML elements designed to take a specific form of input from users. Different types of input elements can regulate the data entered to fit a specified format and provide security to password entry.

Section 17.1: Text

The most basic input type and the default input if no type is specified. This input type defines a single-line text field with line-breaks automatically removed from the input value. All other characters can be entered into this. **<input>** elements are used within a **<form>** element to declare input controls that allow users to input data.

Syntax
<input   type="text"**>**
or (without specifying a type, using the default attribute):

<input>
The default width of a text field input is 20 characters. This can be changed by specifying a value for the size attribute like this: **<input** type="text" size="50"**>**

The size attribute is distinctly different than setting a width with CSS. Using a width defines a specific value (in number of pixel, percentage of the parent element, etc.) that the input must always be wide. Using the size calculates the amount of width to allocate based on the font being used and how wide the characters normally are.

Note: Using the size attribute does not inherently limit the number of characters which can be entered into the box, only how wide the box is displayed. For limiting the length, see Input   Validation.
An input field only allows one line of text. If you need a multi-line text input for substantial amount of text, use a **<textarea>** element instead.

Section 17.2: Checkbox and Radio Buttons
Overview

Checkboxes and radio buttons are written with the HTML tag **<input>**, and their behavior is defined in the HTML specification.

The simplest checkbox or radio button is an **<input>** element with a type attribute of checkbox or radio, respectively:

```
<input                    type="checkbox">
<input type="radio">
```

A single stand-alone checkbox element is used for a single binary option such as a yes-or-no question. Checkboxes are independent, meaning the user may select as many choices as they would like in a group of checkboxes. In other words, checking one checkbox does *not* uncheck the other checkboxes in checkbox group.

Radio buttons usually come in groups (if it's not grouped with another radio button, you probably meant to use a checkbox instead) identified by using the same name attribute on all buttons within that group. The selection of radio buttons are *mutually exclusive*, meaning the user may only select one choice from a group of radio buttons. When a radio button is checked, any other radio button with the same name that was previously checked becomes unchecked.

Example:

```
<input    type="radio"  name="color"  id="red"
value="#F00"> <input type="radio" name="color"
id="green"  value="#0F0"> <input  type="radio"
name="color" id="blue" value="#00F">
```

81

When viewed, radio buttons appear as a circle (unchecked) or a filled circle (checked). Checkboxes appear as a square (unchecked) or a filled square (checked). Depending on the browser and operating system, the square sometimes has rounded corners.

Attributes
checkboxes and radio buttons have a number of attributes to control their behavior:
value

Like any other input element, the value attribute specifies the string value to associate with the button in the event of form submission. However, checkboxes and radio buttons are special in that when the value is omitted, it defaults to on when submitted, rather than sending a blank value. The value attribute is not reflected in the button's appearance.

checked

The checked attribute specifies the initial state of a checkbox or radio button. This is a boolean attribute and may be omitted. Each of these are valid, equivalent ways to define a checked radio button:

```
<input                          checked>
<input                          checked="">
```

<input checked="checked"**>** **<input** checked="ChEcKeD"**>**

The absence of the checked attribute is the only valid syntax for an unchecked button: **<input** type="radio"**>** **<input** type="checkbox"**>** When resetting a **<form>**, checkboxes and radio buttons revert to the state of their checked attribute.

Accessibility Labels

To give context to the buttons and show users what each button is for, each of them should have a label. This can be done using a **<label>** element to wrap the button. Also, this makes the label clickable, so you select the corresponding button.

Example:

<label>
<input type="radio" name="color" value="#F00"**>** Red

</label>
or with a **<label>** element with a for attribute set to the id attribute of the button: **<input** type="checkbox" name="color" value="#F00" id="red"**>** **<label** for="red"**>**Red**</label>**

Button **Groups**

Since each radio button affects the others in the group, it is common to provide a label or context for the entire group of radio buttons. To provide a label for the entire group, the radio buttons should be included in a **<fieldset>** element with a **<legend>** element within it. Example:

```
<fieldset>
<legend>Theme              color:</legend>
<p>

<input type="radio" name="color" id="red" value="#F00">  <label for="red">Red</label>
</p>
<p>
<input type="radio" name="color" id="green" value="#0F0">
<label                for="green">Green</label>
</p>
<p>
<input type="radio" name="color" id="blue" value="#00F">
<label                for="blue">Blue</label>
</p>
</fieldset>
```

Checkboxes can also be grouped in a similar fashion, with a fieldset and legend identifying the group of related checkboxes. However, keep in mind that checkboxes should *not* share the same name because they are not mutually exclusive. Doing this will result in the form submitting multiple values for the same key and not all serverside languages handle this in the same way (undefined behavior). Each checkbox should either have a unique name, or use a set of square brackets ([]) to indicate that the form should submit an array of values for that key. Which method you choose should depend on how you plan to handle the form data client-side or server-side. You should also keep the legend short, since some combinations of browsers and screen readers read the legend before each input field in the fieldset.

Section 17.3: Input Validation

HTML input validation is done automatically by the browser based on special attributes on the input element. It could partially or completely replace JavaScript input validation. This kind of validation can be circumvented by the user via specially crafted HTTP requests, so it does not replace server-side input validation. The validation only occurs when attempting to submit the form, so all restricted inputs must be inside a form in order for validation to occur (unless you're using JavaScript). Keep in mind that inputs which are disabled or read-only will not trigger validation.

Some newer input types (like email, url, tel, date and many more) are automatically validated and do not require your own validation constraints. Version ≥ 5 **Required** Use the required attribute to indicate that a field must be completed in order to pass validation.

<input required**>** **Minimum / Maximum Length**

Use the minlength and maxlength attributes to indicate length requirements. Most browsers will prevent the user from typing more than *max* characters into the box, preventing them from making their entry invalid even before they attempt submission.

<input minlength="3"**>**
 <input maxlength="15"**>**
 <input minlength="3" maxlength="15"**>**

Specifying a range
Use min and max attributes to restrict the range of numbers a user can input into an input of type number or range Marks: **<input** type="number" size="6" name="marks" min="0" max="100" /> Subject Feedback: **<input** type="range" size="2" name="feedback" min="1" max="5" /> Version ≥ 5

Match a **Pattern**

For more control, use the pattern attribute to specify any regular expression that must be matched in order to pass validation. You can also specify a title, which is included in the validation message if the field doesn't pass.
<input pattern="\d*" title="Numbers only, please."**>**

Here's the message shown in Google Chrome version 51 when attempting to submit the form with an invalid value inside this field:

Not all browsers display a message for invalid patterns, although there is full support among most used modern browsers. Check the latest support on CanIUse and implement accordingly.

Version ≥ 5

Accept **File** **Type**

For input fields of type file, it is possible to accept only certain types of files, such as videos, images, audios, specific file extensions, or certain media types. For example:
<input type="file" accept="image/*"

title="Only images are allowed">
Multiple values can be specified with a comma, e.g.:

```
<input                          type="file"
accept="image/*,.rar,application/zip">
```

Note: Adding novalidate attribute to the form element or formnovalidate attribute to the submit button, prevents validation on form elements. For example:

```
<form>
<input   type="text"   name="name"   required>
<input   type="email"   name="email"   required>
<input pattern="\d*" name="number" required>

<input   type="submit"   value="Publish">   <!--
form       will       be       validated       -->
<input       type="submit"       value="Save"
formnovalidate> <!-- form will NOT be validated
-->                                          </form>
```

The form has fields that are required for "publishing" the draft but aren't required for "saving" the draft.

Section 17.4: Color
Version ≥ 5

```
<input      type="color"      name="favcolor"
value="#ff0000">
```

In supporting browsers, the input element with a type attribute whose value is color creates a button-like control, with a color equal to the value of color attribute (defaults to black if value is not specified or is an invalid hexadecimal format).

Clicking this button opens the operating system's color widget, which allows user to select a color.

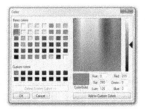

Fallback for browsers which do not support this input type is a regular input type=text.

Section 17.5: Password
<input
type="password"   name="password">
The input element with a type attribute whose value is password creates a single-line text field similar to the input type=text, except that text is not displayed as the user enters it.

```
<input   type="password"   name="password"
placeholder="Password">
```
Placeholder text is shown in plain text and is overwritten automatically when a user starts typing.

Password

Note: Some browsers and systems modify the default behavior of the password field to also display the most recently typed character for a short duration, like so:

••r

Section 17.6: File

```
<input
type="file"                name="fileSubmission">
```

File inputs allow users to select a file from their local filesystem for use with the current page. If used in conjunction with a form element, they can be used to allow users to upload files to a server (for more info see Uploading Files).
The following example allows users to use the file input to select a file from their filesystem and upload that file to a script on the server named upload_file.php.

```
< form action="upload_file.php" method="post"
enctype="multipart/form-data">
Select         file         to         upload:
<input     type="file"     name="fileSubmission"
id="fileSubmission">
```

```html
<input type="submit" value="Upload your file" name="submit">
```

```html
</form>
```

Multiple   **files**

Adding the multiple attribute the user will be able to select **more than one** file:

```html
<input type="file" name="fileSubmission" id="fileSubmission" multiple>
```

Accept   **Files**

Accept attribute specifies the types of files that user can select. E.g. .png, .gif, .jpeg.
```html
<input type="file" name="fileSubmission" accept="image/x-png,image/gif,image/jpeg" />
```

Section 17.7: Button

```html
<input type="button" value="Button Text">
```
Buttons can be used for triggering actions to occur on the page, without submitting the form. You can also use the **<button>** element if you require a button that can be more easily styled or contain other elements:
```html
<button type="button">Button Text</button>
```
Buttons are typically used with an "onclick" event:
```html
<input type="button" onclick="alert('hello world!')" value="Click Me">
```
or
```html
<button type="button" onclick="alert('hello world!')">Click Me</button>
```

91

Attributes   **[name]**
The name of the button, which is submitted with the form data.

[type]
The type of the button.
Possible   values   are:
submit : The button submits the form data to the server. This is the default if the attribute is not specified, or if the attribute is dynamically changed to an empty or invalid value.
reset : The button resets all the controls to their initial values.
button : The button has no default behavior. It can have client-side scripts associated with the element's events, which are triggered when the events occur.
menu : The button opens a popup menu defined via its designated element.

[value]
The initial value of the button.
Version   ≥   5
Extra Attributes for Submit Buttons Attribute
form
formaction
formenctype
formmethod

Description
Specifies the ID of the form the button belongs to.

If none is specified, it will belong to its ancestor form element (if one exists).

Specifies where to send the form-data when the form is submitted using this button.

Specifies how the form-data should be encoded when submitting it to the server using this button.
Can only be used with formmethod="post".

Specifies the HTTP method to use (POST or GET)
when sending form-data using this button. formnovalidateSpecifies that the form-data should not be validated on submission. Specifies where to display the response that is received_{formtarget} after submitting the form using this button.

Section 17.8: Submit
<input
type="submit"   value="Submit">
A submit input creates a button which submits the form it is inside when clicked. You can also use the **<button>** element if you require a submit button that can be more easily styled or contain other elements:

<button   type="submit">
<img   src="submit-icon.jpg"   **/>**   Submit
</button>

93

Section 17.9: Reset

<input
  type="reset"   value="Reset"**>**
An input of type reset creates a button which, when clicked, resets all inputs in the form it is contained in to their default state.

Text in an input field will be reset to blank or its default value (specified using the value attribute). Any option(s) in a selection menu will be deselected unless they have the selected attribute. All checkboxes and radio boxes will be deselected unless they have the checked attribute.

Note: A reset button must be inside or attached to (via the form attribute) a **<form>** element in order to have any effect. The button will only reset the elements within this form.

Section 17.10: Hidden

<input
  type="hidden"   name="inputName"
value="inputValue"**>**
A hidden input won't be visible to the user, but its value will be sent to the server when the form is submitted nonetheless.

Section 17.11: Tel

<input

type="tel"   value="+8400000000">
The input element with a type attribute whose value is tel represents a one-line plain-text edit control for entering a telephone number.

Section 17.12: Email
Version ≥ 5

The **<input** type="email"**>** is used for input fields that should contain an e-mail address.

<form>
<label>E-mail: **<label>**
<input type="email" name="email"**>**

</form>
E-mail address can be automatically validated when submitted depending on browser support.

Section 17.13: Number
Version ≥ 5

<input   type="number"   value="0" name="quantity"**>**
The Input element with a type attribute whose value is number represents a precise control for setting the element's value to a string representing a number.
Please note that this field does not guarantee to have a correct number. It just allows all the

symbols which could be used in any real number, for example user will be able to enter value like e1e-,0.

Section 17.14: Range
Version ≥ 5

`<input type="range" min="" max="" step="" />`
A control for entering a number whose exact value is not important.

Attribute Description Default value min Minimum value for range 0 max Maximum value for range 100 step Amount to increase by on each increment. 1

Section 17.15: Search
Version ≥ 5

Input type search is used for textual search. It will add magnifier symbol next to space for text on most browsers `<input type="search" name="googlesearch">`

Section 17.16: Image
`<input type="image" src="img.png" alt="image_name" height="50px" width="50px"/>`
An Image. You must use the src attribute to

define the source of the image and the alt attribute to define alternative text. You can use the height and width attributes to define the size of the image in pixels.

Section 17.17: Week
Version ≥ 5

<input type="week" **/>**
Dependent on browser support, a control will show for entering a week-year number and a week number with no time zone.

Section 17.18: Url
Version ≥ 5

<input type="url" name="Homepage"**>**
This is used for input fields that should contain a URL address. Depending on browser support, the url field can be automatically validated when submitted. Some smartphones recognize the url type, and adds ".com" to the keyboard to match url input.

Section 17.19: DateTime-Local
Version ≥ 5

<input type="datetime-local" **/>**
Dependent on browser support, a date and time picker will pop up on screen for you to choose a date and time.

Section 17.20: Month
Version ≥ 5

<input type="month" **/>**
Dependent on browser support, a control will show to pick the month.

Section 17.21: Time
Version ≥ 5

<input type="time" **/>**
The time input marks this element as accepting a string representing a time. The format is defined in RFC 3339 and should be a partial-time such as

 19:04:39
 08:20:39.04

Currently, all versions of Edge, Chrome, Opera, and Chrome for Android support type="time". The newer versions of Android Browser, specifically 4.4 and up support it. Safari for iOS offers partial support, not supporting min, max, and step attributes.

Section 17.22: DateTime (Global)
The input element with a type attribute whose value is "**datetime**" represents a control for setting the element's value to a string

representing a **global date and time (with timezone information).**

<fieldset>
<p><label>Meeting time: **<input** type=datetime name="meeting.start"**></label>**
</fieldset>

Permitted attributes:

global	attributes	name
disabled		
form		
type		
autocomplete		autofocus
list		
min	&	max
step		(float)
readonly		
required value		

Section 17.23: Date
Version ≥ 5

<input type="date" **/>**
A date picker will pop up on screen for you to choose a date. This is not supported in Firefox or Internet Explorer.

Chapter 18: Forms

Attribute

accept-charset   action
autocomplete

enctype

method
name
novalidate target

Description

Specifies the character encodings that are to be used for the form submission. Specifies where to send the form-data when a form is submitted. Specifies whether a form should have autocomplete on or off. Specifies how the form-data should be encoded when submitting it to the server (only for method="post").

Specifies the HTTP method to use when sending form-data (POST or GET). Specifies the name of a form.

Specifies that the form should not be validated when submitted. Specifies where to display the response that is received after submitting the form.

In order to group input elements and submit data, HTML uses a form element to encapsulate input and submission elements. These forms handle sending the data in the specified method to a page handled by a server or handler. This topic explains and demonstrates the usage of HTML forms in collecting and submitting input data.

Section 18.1: Submitting
The Action Attribute

The action attribute defines the action to be performed when the form is submitted, which usually leads to a script that collects the information submitted and works with it. if you leave it blank, it will send it to the same file

<form   action="action.php">

The   Method   Attribute
The method attribute is used to define the HTTP method of the form which is either GET or POST.

<form   action="action.php"   method="get">
<form   action="action.php"   method="post">
The GET method is mostly used to *get* data, for example to receive a post by its ID or name, or to submit a search query. The GET method will append the form data to the URL specified in the action   attribute.

www.example.com/action.php?firstname=Mickey&lastname=Mouse
The POST method is used when submitting data to a script. The POST method does not append the form data to the action URL but sends using the request body.
To submit the data from the form correctly, a name attribute name must be specified. As an example let's send the value of the field and set its name to *lastname*:
<input type="text" name="lastname" value="Mouse"**>**

More   attributes
<**form** action="action.php" method="post" target="_blank" accept-charset="UTF-8" enctype="application/x-www-form-urlencoded" autocomplete="off" novalidate>
<!-- form elements --> </**form**>

Section 18.2: Target attribute in form tag
The target attribute specifies a name or a keyword that indicates where to display the response that is received after submitting the form.
The target attribute defines a name of, or keyword for, a browsing context (e.g. tab, window, or inline frame).
From Tag with a target attribute:
<form target="_blank"**>**
Attribute Values

102

Value	Description
_blank	The response is displayed in a new window or tab
_self	The response is displayed in the same frame (this is default)
_parent	The response is displayed in the parent frame
_top	The response is displayed in the full body of the window
framename	The response is displayed in a named iframe

Note: The target attribute was **deprecated** in **HTML 4.01**. The target attribute is **supported** in **HTML5**.

Frames and framesets are not supported in **HTML5**, so the **_parent, _top and framename values are now mostly used with iframes**.

Section 18.3: Uploading Files

Images and files can be uploaded/submitted to server by setting enctype attribute of form tag to multipart/formdata. enctype specifies how form data would be encoded while submitting to the server.

Example

```
< form method="post" enctype="multipart/form-
data" action="upload.php"> <input type="file"
name="pic"                                  />
<input type="submit" value="Upload" />
```

103

</**form**>

Section 18.4: Grouping a few input fields
While designing a form, you might like to group a few input fields into a group to help organise the form layout. This can be done by using the tag . Here is an example for using it. For each fieldset, you can set a legend for the set using the tag LEGEND TEXT
Example

<form>
<fieldset>
<legend>1st field set:**</legend>**
Field one:**
**
<input type="text"**>
**

Field two: **
**
<input type="text"**>
**
**</fieldset>
**
<fieldset>
<legend>2nd field set:**</legend>**
Field three:**
**
<input type="text"**>
**
Field four:**
**
<input type="text"**>
**
**</fieldset>
**
<input type="submit" value="Submit"**> </form>**

Result

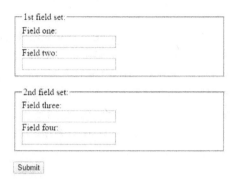

Browser   **Support**

Chrome, IE, Edge, FireFox, Safari and Opera's latest versions also supports the tag

Chapter 19: Div Element

The div element in HTML is a container element that encapsulates other elements and can be used to group and separate parts of a webpage. A div by itself does not inherently represent anything but is a powerful tool in web design. This topic covers the purpose and applications of the div element.

Section 19.1: Basic usage

The **<div>** element usually has no specific semantic meaning by itself, simply representing a division, and is typically used for grouping and encapsulating other elements within an HTML document and separating those from other groups of content. As such, each **<div>** is best described by its contents.

<div>
<p>Hello!   This   is   a   paragraph.**</p>**
</div>

The div element is typically a block-level element, meaning that it separates a block of an HTML document and occupying the maximum width of the page. Browsers typically have the following default CSS rule:

```
div                                        {
  display:                             block;
}
```

It's strongly encouraged by the **The World Wide Web Consortium (W3C)** to view the div element as an element of last resort, for when no other element is suitable. The use of more appropriate elements instead of the div element leads to better accessibility for readers and easier maintainability for authors.

For example, a blog post would be marked up using **<article>**, a chapter using **<section>**, a page's navigation aids using **<nav>**, and a group of form controls using **<fieldset>**. div elements can be useful for stylistic purposes or to wrap multiple paragraphs within a section that are all to be annotated in a similar way.

Section 19.2: Nesting
It is a common practice to place multiple **<div>** inside another **<div>**. This is usually referred to as "nesting" elements and allows for further dividing elements into subsections or aid developers with CSS styling. The **<div** class="outer-div"**>** is used to group together two **<div** class="inner-div"**>** elements; each containing a **<p>** element.

```
<div                                class="outer-div">
<div class="inner-div">

<p>      This      is      a      paragraph</p>
</div>
<div class="inner-div">

<p>This      is      another      paragraph</p>
</div>
</div>
```

This will yield the following result (CSS styles applied for clarity):

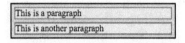

Nesting inline and block elements While nesting elements you should keep in mind, that there are inline and block elements. while block elements "add a line break in the background", what means, other nested elements are shown in the next line automatically, inline elements can be positioned next to each other by default

Avoid   deep   <div>   nesting
A deep and oftenly used nested container layouts shows a bad coding style.

Rounded corners or some similar functions often create such an HTML code. For most of the last generation browsers there are CSS3 counterparts.

108

Try to use as little as possible HTML elements to increase the content to tag ratio and reduce page load, resulting in a better ranking in search engines.

div section Element should be not nested deeper than 6 layers.

Chapter 20: Sectioning Elements

Section 20.1: Nav Element

The **<nav>** element is primarily intended to be used for sections that contain **main navigation blocks** for the website, this can include links to other parts of the web page *(e.g. anchors for a table of contents)* or other pages entirely.

Inline **items**
The following will display an inline set of hyperlinks.

<nav>
<a href="https://google.com"**>**Google**</a>**
<a href="https://www.yahoo.com"**>**Yahoo!**</a>**
<a href="https://www.bing.com"**>**Bing**</a>**

</nav>
Use **list** **items** **when** **needed**
If the content represents a list of items, use a

list item to show this and enhance the user experience.

Note the role="navigation", *more on this below.*

```
<nav                    role="navigation">
 <ul>
 <li><a
href="https://google.com">Google</a></li>
<li><a
href="https://www.yahoo.com">Yahoo!</a></li>
<li><a
href="https://www.bing.com">Bing</a></li>

 </ul>
 </nav>
```

Avoid   unnecessary   usage   <footer> elements may have a list of links to other parts of the site (FAQ, T&C, etc.). The footer element alone is sufficient in this case, you don't *need* to further wrap your links with a **<nav>** element in the **<footer>**.

```
 <!-- the <nav> is not required in the <footer> -
> <footer>

<nav>
 <a                        href="#">...</a>
 </nav>
 </footer>
```

```
<!-- The footer alone is sufficient -> <footer>
<a                    href="#">...</a>
</footer>
```
Notes:

<main> element descendants are not allowed within a **<nav>**

Adding a role="navigation"ARIA role to the **<nav>** element is advised to aid user agents that don't support HTML5 and also to provide more context for those that do.
<nav role="navigation"><!-- ... -></nav>

Screen Readers:_(software that allows blind or visually impaired users to navigate the site)_

User agents like screen readers will interpret the **<nav>** element differently depending on their requirements.

It could give the **<nav>** element a higher priority when rendering the page
It could delay the rendering of the element
It could adapt the page in a specific way to tailor for the user's needs
example: make the text links within the **<nav>** elements larger for someone who's visually impaired.

Click here to read the official HTML5 Specification for the **<nav>** element

Section 20.2: Article Element

111

The **<article>** element contains **self-contained content** like articles, blog posts, user comments or an interactive widget that could be distributed outside the context of the page, for example by RSS.
When article elements are nested, the contents of the inner article node should be related to the outer article element.
A blog (section) with multiple posts (article), and comments (article) might look something like this.

<section>
<!-- Each individual blog post is an <article> -->
<article>

<header>
<h1>Blog Post**</h1>**
<time datetime="2016-03-13"**>**13th March 2016**</time>**

</header>
<p>The article element represents a self contained article or document.**</p>** **<p>**The section element represents a grouping of content.**</p>**
<section>
<h2>Comments **<small>**relating to "Blog Post"**</small></h2>**

<!-- Related comment is also a self-contained article -->
```html
<article id="user-comment-1">
<p>Excellent!</p>
<footer><p>...</p><time>...</time></footer>
</article>
</section>
</article>

<!-- ./repeat: <article> -->

</section>
<!-- Content unrelated to the blog or posts should be outside the section. --> <footer>
<p>This content should be unrelated to the blog.</p>
</footer>
```

Avoid unnecessary usage

When the main content of the page (excluding headers, footers, navigation bars, etc.) is simply one group of elements. You can omit the **<article>** in favour of the **<main>** element.

```html
<article>
<p>This doesn't make sense, this article has no real `context`.</p>
</article>
```

Instead, replace the article with a **<main>** element to indicate this is the main content for this page.

113

```
<main>
<p>I'm the main content, I don't need to belong
to                    an                    article.</p>
</main>
```

If you use another element, ensure you specify
the **<main>** ARIA role for correct interpretation
and rendering across multiple devices and non
HTML5 browsers.

```
<section                          role="main">
<p>This section is the main content of this
page.</p>
</section>
```

Notes:
<main> element descendants are not allowed
within a **<article>** Click here to read the official
HTML5 Specification for the **<article>**
element

Section 20.3: Main Element

The **<main>** element contains the **main content**
for your web page. This content is unique to the
individual page, and should not appear elsewhere
on the site. Repeating content like headers,
footers, navigation, logos, etc., is placed outside
the element.

The **<main>** element should only ever be used at most **once** on a single page. The **<main>** element must not be included as a descendant of an article, aside, footer, header or nav element.

In the following example, we're displaying a **single blog post** (and related information like references and comments).

```
<body>
<header>
<nav>...</nav>
</header>

<main>
<h1>Individual Blog Post</h1>
<p>An introduction for the post.</p>

<article>
<h2>References</h2>
<p>...</p>

</article>
<article>
<h2>Comments</h2>    ...    </article>
</main>
<footer>...</footer>    </body>
```

The blog post is contained within the **<main>** element to indicate this is the main content for this page (and therefore, unique across the website).

The **<header>** and **<footer>** tags are *siblings* to the **<main>** element.

Notes:

The HTML5 specification recognizes the **<main>** element as a **grouping** element, and not a *sectioning* element. ARIA role attributes: main*(default)*, presentation

Adding a role="main"ARIA role attribute to **other elements** intended to be used as main content is advised to aid user agents that don't support HTML5 and also to provide more context for those that do. The **<main>** element by default has the main role, and so does not need to be provided. Click here to read the official HTML5 Specification for the **<main>** element

Section 20.4: Header Element

The **<header>** element represents introductory content for its nearest ancestor sectioning content or sectioning root element. A **<header>** typically contains a group of introductory or navigational aids.

Note: The header element is not sectioning content; it doesn't introduce a new section.

Examples:

<header>
<p>Welcome to...**</p>** **<h1>**Voidwars!**</h1>**

116

</header>
In this example, the **<article>** has a **<header>**.
<article>
<header>

<h1> Flexbox: The definitive guide**</h1>**
</header>
<p>The guide about Flexbox was supposed to be here, but it turned out Wes wasn't a Flexbox expert

either.**</p>**
</article>

Section 20.5: Footer Element
The **<footer>** element contains the footer part of the page.
Here is an example for **<footer>** element that contain p paragraph tag.

<footer>
<p>All rights reserved**</p>**
</footer>

Section 20.6: Section Element
The **<section>** element represents a generic section to thematically group content. Every section, typically, should be able to be

117

identified with a heading element as a child of the section.

You can use the **<section>** element within an **<article>** and vice-versa. Every section should have a *theme* (a heading element identifying this region) Don't use the **<section>** element as a general styling 'container'. If you need a container to apply styling, use a **<div>** instead.

In the following example, we're displaying a **single blog post** with multiple chapters each chapter is a section *(a set of thematically grouped content, which can be identified by the heading elements in each section).*

```
<article>
<header>
<h2>                    Blog                    Post</h2>
</header>
<p>An introduction for the post.</p> <section>
<h3>                    Chapter                    1</h3>
<p>...</p>
</section>
<section>
<h3>Chapter                    2</h3>
<p>...</p>
</section>
```

```
<section>
<h3>Comments</h3>                           ...
</section>
</article>
```

Notes:

Developers should use the **article** element when it makes sense to syndicate the contents of the element. Click here to read the official HTML5 Specification for the **<main>** element

Chapter 21: Navigation Bars

Section 21.1: Basic Navigation Bar
Navigation bars are essentially a list of links, so the ul and li elements are used to encase navigation links.

```
<ul>
<li><a                    href="#">Home</a></li>
<li><a                    href="#">About</a></li>
<li><a href="#">Contact</a></li>

</ul>
```

Section 21.2: HTML5 Navigation Bar
To make a navigation bar using the HTML5 nav element, encase the links within the nav tag.

```
<nav>
<a                        href="#">Home</a>
<a                        href="#">About</a>
<a href="#">Contact</a>

</nav>
```

Chapter 22: Label Element

Attributes Description

for Reference to the target ID Element. I.e: for="surname"

HTML5 , **[Obsolete]** Reference to the form containing the Target Element. Label elements are expected form within a **<form>** Element. If the form="someFormId" is provided this allows you to place the Label anywhere in the document.

Section 22.1: About Label
The **<label>** element is used to reference a form action element.
In the scope of **User Interface** it's used to ease the target / selection of elements like Type radio or checkbox.
<label> **as** **wrapper**
It can enclose the desired action element

<label>
<input type="checkbox" name="Cats">
I like Cats!

</label>
(Clicking on the text the target input will toggle it's state / value)
<label> **as** **reference**
Using the for attribute you don't have to place the control element as descendant of label - but

the for value must match it's ID
```
<input          id="cats"          type="checkbox"
name="Cats">    <label  for="cats"   >I    like
Cats!</label>
```
Note
Don't use more than one Control Element
within a **<label>** element

Section 22.2: Basic Use
Simple   form   with   labels...
```
<form     action="/login"     method="POST">
<label     for="username">Username:</label>
<input          id="username"          type="text"
name="username"                              />
<label           for="pass">Password:</label>
<input          id="pass"          type="password"
name="pass"                                  />
<input   type="submit"   name="submit"   />
</form>
```
Version   ≥   5
```
<form     id="my-form"     action="/login"
method="POST">
<input          id="username"          type="text"
name="username"                              />
<label           for="pass">Password:</label>
<input          id="pass"          type="password"
name="pass"                                  />
<input   type="submit"   name="submit"   />
</form>    <label  for="username"  form="my-
form">Username:</label>
```

Chapter 23: Output Element

Attribute Description

Global
Attributes that are available to any HTML5 element. For comprehensive documentation of these attributes see: MDN Global Attributes

name
A string representing the name of an output. As a form element, output can be referenced by it's name using the document.forms property. This attribute is also used for collecting values on a form submit.

for
A space separated list of form element ids (e.g. **<inputs** id="inp1"**>** for value is "inp1") that the output is meant to display calculations for. A string representing the **<form>** that is associated to the output. If the output is actually outside the

form **<form>**, this attribute will ensure that the output still belongs to the **<form>** and subject to collections and submits of said **<form>**.

Section 23.1: Output Element Using For and Form Attributes

124

The following demo features an **<output>** element's use of the [for] and [form] attributes. Keep in mind, **<output> needs JavaScript** in order to function. Inline JavaScript is commonly used in forms as this example demonstrates. Although the **<input>** elements are type="number", their values are not numbers, they are text. So if you require the values to be calculated, you must convert each value into a number using methods such as: parseInt(), parseFloat(), Number(), etc.

Live Demo

```
<!--form1 will collect the values of in1 and in2
on 'input' event.--> <!--out1 value will be the
sum of in1 and in2 values.-->
<form id="form1" name="form1"
oninput="out1.value = parseInt(in1.value, 10) +
parseInt(in2.value, 10)">
  <fieldset>
  <legend>Output Example</legend>

<input type="number" id="in1" name="in1"
value="0">                                    <br/>
  +
<input type="number" id="in2" name="in2"
value="0">

  </fieldset>
  </form>
  <!--[for] attribute enables out1 to display
```

125

calculations for in1 and in2.--> *<!--[form] attribute designates form1 as the form owner of out1 even if it isn't a descendant.-->* **<output** name="out1" for="in1 in2" form="form1"**>0</output>**

Section 23.2: Output Element with Attributes
<output
 name="out1" form="form1" for="inp1 inp2"**></output>**

Chapter 24: Void Elements

Not all HTML tags are of the same structure. While most elements require an opening tag, a closing tag, and contents, some elements - known as void elements - only require an opening tag as they themselves do not contain any elements. This topic explains and demonstrates the proper usage of void elements in HTML

Section 24.1: Void elements
HTML 4.01/XHTML 1.0 Strict includes the following void elements:

area - clickable, defined area in an image
base - specifies a base URL from which all links base
br   -   line   break

col - column in a table [deprecated]
hr - horizontal rule (line)
img - image
input - field where users enter data
link - links an external resource to the document
meta - provides information about the document
param - defines parameters for plugins

HTML 5 standards include all non-deprecated tags from the previous list and

command - represents a command users can invoke [obsolete] keygen - facilitates public key generation for web certificates [deprecated] source - specifies media sources for picture, audio, and video elements

The example below does **not** include void elements:
<div>
<a href="http://stackoverflow.com/">

<h3> Click here to visit **<i>**Stack Overflow!**</i></h3>** **</a>**
<button> onclick="alert('Hello!');">Say Hello!**</button>** **<p>**My favorite language is ****HTML****. Here are my others:**</p> <ol>**

<li> CSS**</li>**
<li>JavaScript**</li> <li>**PHP**</li>**

```
</ol>
</div>
```
Notice how every element has an opening tag, a closing tag, and text or other elements inside the opening and closing tags. Void tags however, are shown in the example below:

```
<img src="https://cdn.sstatic.net/Sites/stackoverflow/company/img/logos/so/so-icon.png" /> <br>
<hr>
<input type="number" placeholder="Enter your favorite number">
```

With the exception of the img tag, all of these void elements have only an opening tag. The img tag, unlike any other tag, has a self closing / before the greater than sign of the opening tag. It is best practice to have a space before the slash.

Chapter 25: Media Elements

Attribute	Details
width	Sets the element's width in pixels.
height	Sets the element's height in pixels.
<source>	Defines resources of the audio or video files
track	Defines the text track for media elements
controls	Displays controls

autoplay Automatically start playing the media
loop Plays the media in a repeated cycle
muted Plays the media without sound
poster Assigns an image to display until a video is loaded

Section 25.1: Audio

HTML5 provides a new standard for embedding an audio file on a web page. You can embed an audio file to a page using the **<audio>** element:

<audio   controls>
 <source src="file.mp3" type="audio/mpeg">
Your browser does not support the audio element.
 </audio>

Section 25.2: Video

You can embed also a video to a webpage using the **<video>** element:

<video width="500" height="700" controls>
 <source src="video.mp4" type="video/mp4">
Your browser does not support the video tag.
 </video>

Section 25.3: Using `<video>` and `<audio>` element to display audio/video content

Use the HTML or **<audio>** element to embed video/audio content in a document. The video/audio element contains one or more video/audio sources. To specify a source, use either the src attribute or the **<source>** element; the browser will choose the most suitable one.

Audio tag example:

```
<!-- Simple video example ->
<video src="videofile.webm" autoplay poster="posterimage.jpg"> Sorry, your browser doesn't support embedded videos, but don't worry, you can <a href="videofile.webm">download it</a> and watch it with your favorite video player! </video>
```

```
<!-- Video with subtitles ->
<video src="foo.webm">
<track kind="subtitles" src="foo.en.vtt" srclang="en" label="English"> <track kind="subtitles" src="foo.sv.vtt" srclang="sv" label="Svenska">

</video>
```

```
<!-- Simple video example ->
<video width="480" controls poster="https://archive.org/download/WebmVp8Vorbis/webmvp8.gif" >
```

```html
<source
src="https://archive.org/download/WebmVp8Vor
bis/webmvp8.webm"          type="video/webm">
<source
src="https://archive.org/download/WebmVp8Vor
bis/webmvp8_512kb.mp4"    type="video/mp4">
<source
src="https://archive.org/download/WebmVp8Vor
bis/webmvp8.ogv"        type="video/ogg">    Your
browser doesn't support HTML5 video tag.

</video>
Audio              tag              example:
<!--    Simple    audio    playback    ->
<audio
src="http://developer.mozilla.org/@api/deki/fil
es/2926/=AudioTest_(1).ogg" autoplay>    Your
browser    does    not    support    the
<code>audio</code>                   element.
</audio>


<!--    Audio    playback    with    captions    ->
<audio                           src="foo.ogg">
<track      kind="captions"      src="foo.en.vtt"
srclang="en"       label="English">       <track
kind="captions"    src="foo.sv.vtt"    srclang="sv"
label="Svenska">
</audio>
```

Section 25.4: Video header or background
```
```

Adding a video that will autoplay on a loop and has no controls or sound. Perfect for a video header or background.

```
<video width="1280" height="720" autoplay muted loop poster="video.jpg" id="videobg">
<source src="video.mp4" type="video/mp4">
 <source src="video.webm" type="video/webm">
 <source src="video.ogg" type="video/ogg">

</video>
```

This CSS provides a fallback if the video cannot be loaded. Note that is it recomended to use the first frame of the video as the poster video.jpg.

```
#videobg                                {
 background:      url(video.jpg)      no-repeat;
background-size: cover;

 }
```

Progress Element

Parameter   max
value
position
labels

Value
How much work the task requires in total
How much of the work has been accomplished

already
This attribute returns the current position of the **<progress>** element This attribute returns a list of **<progress>** element labels (if any)

Section 26.1: Progress

The **<progress>** element is new in HTML5 and is used to represent the progress of a task **<progress** value="22" max="100"**></progress>** This creates a bar filled 22%

Section 26.2: Changing the color of a progress bar

Progress bars can be styled with the progress[value] selector.
This example gives a progress bar a width of 250px and a height of 20px

```
progress                    [value]                    {
width:                                           250px;
height: 20px;

}
```

Progress bars can be especially difficult to style.
Chrome / Safari / Opera
These browsers use the -webkit-appearance selector to style the progress tag. To override this, we can reset the appearance.

```
progress                [value]              {
  -webkit-appearance:                    none;
  appearance: none;

}
```

Now, we can style the container itself

```
progress       [value]::-webkit-progress-bar      {
  backgroundcolor:                  "green";
}
```

Firefox

Firefox styles the progress bar a little differently. We have to use these styles

```
progress                [value]              {
  -moz-appearance:                     none;
  appearance:                          none;
  border: none; /* Firefox also renders a border */

}
```

Internet   Explorer

Internet Explorer 10+ supports the progress element. However, it does not support the backgroundcolor property. You'll need to use the color property instead.

```
progress[value]              {
  -webkit-appearance:                   none;
  -moz-appearance: none; appearance: none;
  border: none; /* Remove border from Firefox
  */
```

width: 250px;   height: 20px;
color: blue; }

Section 26.3: HTML Fallback

For browsers that do not support the progress element, you can use this as a workaround.

```
<progress         max="100"        value="20">
<div                   class="progress-bar">
<span        style="width:        20%;">Progress:
20%</span>
</div>
</progress>
```

Browsers that support the progress tag will ignore the div nested inside. Legacy browsers which cannot identify the progress tag will render the div instead.

Selection Menu Controls

Section 27.1: Select Menu

The **<select>** element generates a drop-down menu from which the user can choose an option.

```
<select                          name="">
<option             value="1">One</option>
<option             value="2">Two</option>
<option           value="3">Three</option>
<option value="4">Four</option>
```

</select>
Changing the Size

You can change the size of the selection menu with the size attribute. A size of 0 or 1 displays the standard dropdown style menu. A size greater than 1 will convert the drop-down into a box displaying that many lines, with one option per line and a scrollbar in order to scroll through the available options.

<select name="" size="4"**></select>**
Multi-option Selection Menus

By default, users can only select a single option. Adding the multiple attribute allows users to select multiple options at once and submit all selected options with the form. Using the multiple attribute automatically converts the drop-down menu into a box as if it had a size defined. The default size when this occurs is determined by the specific browser you are using, and it is not possible to change it back to a drop-down style menu while allowing multiple selections.

<select name="" multiple**></select>**

When using the multiple attribute, there is a difference between using 0 and 1 for the size, whereas no difference exists when not using the

136

attribute. Using 0 will cause the browser to behave in whatever default manner it is programmed to do. Using 1 will explicitly set the size of the resulting box to only one row high.

Section 27.2: Options

The options inside a selection menu are what the user will be selection. The normal syntax for an option is as follows: **<option>**Some Option**</option>** However, it's important to note that the text inside the **<option>** element itself is not always used, and essentially becomes the default value for attributes which are not specified.

The attributes which control the actual appearance and function of the option are value and label. The label represents the text which will be displayed in the drop-down menu (what you're looking at and will click on to select it). The value represents the text which will be sent along with form submission. If either of these values is omitted, it uses the text inside the element as the value instead. So the example we gave above could be "expanded" to this:

<option label="Some Option" value="Some Option"**>**

Note the omission of the inside text and end tag, which are not required to actually construct an option inside the menu. If they were included, the inside text would be ignored because both attributes are already specified and the text is not needed. However, you probably won't see a lot of people writing them this way. The most common way it's written is with a value that will be sent to the server, along with the inside text which eventually becomes the label attribute, like so:

```
<option                value="option1">Some
Option</option>
```

Selecting an option by default

You can also specify a certain option to be selected in the menu by default by attaching the selected attribute to it. By default, if no option is specified as selected in the menu, the first option in the menu will be selected when rendered. If more than one option has the selected attribute attached, then the last option present in the menu with the attribute will be the one selected by default.

```
<option    value="option1"    selected>Some
option</option>
```

If you're using the attribute in a multi-option selection menu, then all the options with the attribute will be selected by default, and none will be selected if no options have the attribute.

```html
<select                                      multiple>
 <option        value="option1"        selected>Some
option</option>        <option        value="option2"
selected>Some option</option>

</select>
```

Section 27.3: Option Groups

You can neatly group your options within a selection menu in order to provide a more structured layout in a long list of options by using the **`<optgroup>`** element. The syntax is very basic, by simply using the element with a label attribute to identify the title for the group, and containing zero or more options that should be within that group.

```html
<select                                      name="">
 <option              value="milk">Milk</option>
 <optgroup label="Fruits">

<option        value="banana">Bananas</option>
<option
value="strawberry">Strawberries</option>
</optgroup>
 <optgroup     label="Vegetables"     disabled>
 <option           value="carrot">Carrots</option>
 <option        value="zucchini">Zucchini</option>
</optgroup>
 </select>
```

When using option groups, not all options need to be contained within a group. As well, disabling an option group will disable all options within the group, and it is not possible to manually re-enable a single option within a disabled group.

Section 27.4: Datalist

The **<datalist>** tag specifies a list of pre-defined options for an **<input>** element. It provide an "autocomplete" feature on **<input>** elements. Users will see a drop-down list of options as they write.

<input list="Languages"> **<datalist** id="Languages"> **<option** value="PHP"> **<option** value="Perl"> **<option** value="Python"> **<option** value="Ruby"> **<option** value="C+">

</datalist>

Browser   **Support**
Chrome Edge Mozilla Safari Opera 20.0 10.0 4.0 Not Supported 9.0

Embed

Parameters   **Details**
src   Address   of   the   resource
type Type of embedded resource width
Horizontal   dimension
height Vertical dimension

Section 28.1: Basic usage

The embed tag is new in HTML5. This element provides an integration point for an external (typically non-HTML) application or interactive content.

\<embed src="myflash.swf"**\>**

Section 28.2: Defining the MIME type

The MIME type must be defined using the type attribute.

\<embed type="video/mp4" src="video.mp4" width="640" height="480"**\>**

IFrames

Attribute	name
width	
height	
src	
srcdoc	
sandbox	

Details

Sets the element's name, to be used with an a tag to change the iframe's src. Sets the element's width in pixels. Sets the element's height in pixels. Specifies the page that will be displayed in the frame.

Specifies the content that will be displayed in the frame, assuming the browser supports it. The content must be valid HTML. When set, the contents of the iframe is treated as being from a unique origin and features including scripts, plugins, forms and popups will be disabled. Restrictions can be selectively relaxed by adding a space separated list of values. See the table in Remarks for possible values.

allowfullscreenWhether to allow the iframe's contents to use requestFullscreen()

Section 29.1: Basics of an Inline Frame
The term "IFrame" means Inline Frame. It can be used to include another page in your page. This will yield a small frame which shows the exact contents of the base.html.
<iframe src="base.html"**></iframe>**

Section 29.2: Sandboxing
The following embeds an untrusted web page with all restrictions enabled
<iframe sandbox src="http://example.com/"**></iframe>**
To allow the page to run scripts and submit forms, add allow-scripts and allow-forms to the sandbox attribute.
<iframe sandbox="allow-scripts allow-forms" src="http://example.com/"**></iframe>**
If there is untrusted content (such as user

comments) on the same domain as the parent web page, an iframe can be used to disable scripts while still allowing the parent document to interact with it's content using JavaScript.
 <iframe sandbox="allow-same-origin allow-top-navigation"

src="http://example.com/untrusted/comments/page2"**>**
 The parent document can add event listeners and resize the IFrame to fit its contents. This, along with allow-topnavigation, can make the sandboxed iframe appear to be part of parent document.
 This sandbox is not a replacement for sanitizing input but can be used as part of a defense in depth   strategy.
 Also be aware that this sandbox can be subverted by an attacker convincing a user to visit the iframe's source directly. The Content Security Policy HTTP header can be used to mitigate this attack.

Section 29.3: Setting the Frame Size
 The IFrame can be resized using the width and height attributes, where the values are represented in pixels (HTML 4.01 allowed percentage values, but HTML 5 only allows values in CSS pixels).
 <iframe src="base.html" width="800" height="600"**></iframe>**

Section 29.4: Using the "srcdoc" Attribute

The srcdoc attribute can be used (instead of the src attribute) to specify the exact contents of the iframe as a whole HTML document. This will yield an IFrame with the text "IFrames are cool!"

<iframe srcdoc="<p>IFrames are cool!**</p>"></iframe>**

If the srcdoc attribute isn't supported by the browser, the IFrame will instead fall back to using the src attribute, but if both the src and srcdoc attributes are present and supported by the browser, srcdoc takes precedence. **<iframe** srcdoc="<p>Iframes are cool!**</p>"** src="base.html">**</iframe>**

In the above example, if the browser does not support the srcdoc attribute, it will instead display the contents of the base.html page.

Section 29.5: Using Anchors with IFrames

Normally a change of webpage within an Iframe is initiated from with the Iframe, for example, clicking a link inside the Ifame. However, it is possible to change an IFrame's content from outside the IFrame. You can use an anchor tag whose href attribute is set to the desired URL and whose target attribute is set to the iframe's name attribute.

```
<iframe                        src="webpage.html"
name="myIframe"></iframe>
 <a                 href="different_webpage.html"
target="myIframe">Change the Iframe content to
different_webpage.html</a>
```

Content Languages

Section 30.1: Base Document Language
 It's a good practice to declare the primary
language of the document in the html element:
```
<html                                lang="en">
```
If no other lang attribute is specified in the
document, it means that *everything* (i.e.,
element content and attribute text values) is in
that   language.
 If the document contains parts in other
languages, these parts should get their own
lang attributes to "overwrite" the language
declaration.

Section 30.2: Element Language
 The lang attribute is used to specify the
language of element content and attribute text
values:
```
<p lang="en">The content of this element is in
English.</p>
<p lang="en" title="The value of this attribute
is also in English.">The content of this element
is                 in                 English.</p>
```
The language declaration gets inherited:

145

```
<div                                           lang="en">
<p>This element contains English content.</p>
<p title="This attribute, too.">Same with this
element.</p>

</div>
```

Section 30.3: Elements with Multiple Languages
You can "overwrite" a language declaration:
```
<p lang="en">This English sentence contains
the        German        word        <span
lang="de">Hallo</span>.</p>
```

Section 30.4: Regional URLs
It is possible to add the attribute hreflang to
the elements **<a>** and **<area>** that create
hyperlinks. Such it specifies the language of the
linked resource. The language defined must be
a valid BCP 47[1] language tag.

```
<p>
<a                            href="example.org"
hreflang="en">example.org</a> is one of IANA's
example                                 domains.
</p>
```

1. ↑ IETF Network Working Group: RFC 5646
   Tags   for   Identifying   Languages,   IETF,
   September 2009

Section 30.5: Handling Attributes with Di□erent Languages

You can "overwrite" a parent element's language declaration by introducing any element apart from applet, base, basefont, br, frame, frameset, hr, iframe, meta, param, script (of HTML 4.0) with an own lang attribute:

```
<p lang="en" title="An English paragraph">
<span lang="de" title="A German sentence">Hallo Welt!</span>
</p>
```

SVG

SVG stands for Scalable Vector Graphics. SVG is used to define graphics for the Web
The HTML **<svg>** element is a container for SVG graphics.
SVG has several methods for drawing paths, boxes, circles, text, and graphic images.

Section 31.1: Inline SVG

SVG can be written directly into a HTML document. Inline SVG can be styled and manipulated using CSS and JavaScript.

```
<body>
<svg class="attention" xmlns="http://www.w3.org/2000/svg"
xmlns:xlink="http://www.w3.org/1999/xlink"
```

```
viewBox="0        0        1000        1000"        >
<path                                  id="attention"
 d="m571,767l0,-106q0,-8,-5,-13t-12,-5l-108,0q-
7,0,-12,5t-
5,13l0,106q0,8,5,13t12,6l108,0q7,0,12,-6t5
 ,-13Zm-1,-208l10,-257q0,-6,-5,-10q-7,-6,-14,-6l-
122,0q-7,0,-14,6q-5,4,-
5,12l9,255q0,5,6,9t13,3l103,
 0q8,0,13,-3t6,-9Zm-7,-522l428,786q20,35,-1,70q-
10,17,-26,26t-35,10l-858,0q-18,0,-35,-10t-26,-
26q-21
 ,-35,-1,-70l429,-786q9,-17,26,-27t36,-
10t36,10t27,27Z"                                  />
</svg>
</body>
```

The above inline SVG can then be styled using
the corresponding CSS class:

```
.attention                                    {
 fill: red; width: 50px; height: 50px;

 }
```

The result looks like this:

Section 31.2: Embedding external SVG files in
HTML
You can use the **<img>** or **<object>** elements to
embed external SVG elements. Setting the
height and width is optional but is highly

recommended.

Using the image element
<img src="attention.svg" width="50" height="50"**>**

Using **<img>** does not allow you to style the SVG using CSS or manipulate it using JavaScript.

Using the object element
<object type="image/svg+xml" data="attention.svg" width="50" height="50"**>**

Unlike **<img>**, **<object>** directly imports the SVG into the document and therefore it can be manipulated using Javascript and CSS.

Section 31.3: Embedding SVG using CSS

You can add external SVG files using the background-image property, just as you would do with any other image.
HTML:

<div class="attention"**></div>**
CSS:

```
.attention                              {
background-image:         url(attention.svg);
background-size:      100%        100%;
width:                            50px;
height: 50px;

}
```

You can also embed the image directly into a css file using a data url:

background-image:

url(data:image/svg+xml,%3Csvg%20xmlns%3D%2
2http%3A%2F%2Fwww.w3.org%2F2000%2Fsvg%
22%20xmlns%3Axlink
%3D%22http%3A%2F%2Fwww.w3.org%2F1999%
2Fxlink%22%20viewBox%3D%220%200%201000
%201000%22%20%3E%0D%0A%
3Cpath%20id%3D%22attention%22%20d%3D%22
m571%2C767l0%2C-106q0%2C-8%2C-5%2C-13t-
12%2C-5l-108%2C0q-7%25%20%20%20%20%202C0%2C-12%2C5t-
5%2C13l0%2C106q0%2C8%2C5%2C13t12%2C6l1
08%2C0q7%2C0%2C12%2C-6t5%2C-13Zm-1%2C-
208l10%25%20%202C-257q0%2C-6%2C-5%2C-10q-7%2C-
6%2C-14%2C-6l-122%2C0q-7%2C0%2C-14%2C6q-
5%2C4%2C-5%2C12l9%2C255q0%2
C5%2C6%2C9t13%2C3l103%2C0q8%2C0%2C13%
2C-3t6%2C-9Zm-7%2C-
522l428%2C786q20%2C35%2C-1%2C70q-
10%2C17%2%20%20%20%20C-26%2C26t-35%2C10l-858%2C0q-
18%2C0%2C-35%2C-10t-26%2C-26q-21%2C-
35%2C-1%2C-70l429%2C-786q9%2C-17%
2C26%2C-27t36%2C-
10t36%2C10t27%2C27Z%22%20%2F%3E%0D%0A
%3C%2Fsvg%3E);

Canvas

Attribute   **Description**
height   Specifies   the   canvas   height
width Specifies the canvas width

150

Section 32.1: Basic Example

The canvas element was introduced in HTML5 for drawing graphics.

<canvas id="myCanvas"**>**
Cannot display graphic. Canvas is not supported by your browser (IE<9)
</canvas>

The above will create a transparent HTML**<canvas>** element of 300×150 px in size.

You can use the **canvas** element to draw amazing stuff like shapes, graphs, manipulate images, create engaging games etc. with **JavaScript**. The canvas's 2D *drawable layer* surface Object is referred to as CanvasRenderingContext2D; or from a HTMLCanvasElement using the .getContext("2d") method:

var
ctx = document.getElementById("myCanvas").getContext("2d");
// now we can refer to the canvas's 2D layer context using `ctx`
ctx.fillStyle = "#f00";
ctx.fillRect(0, 0, ctx.canvas.width, ctx.canvas.height); *// x, y, width, height*
ctx.fillStyle = "#000";
ctx.fillText("My red canvas with some black

```
text",     24,     32);     //     text,   x,     y
```

jsFiddle example

Section 32.2: Drawing two rectangles on a <canvas>

```html
<!DOCTYPE                                      html>
<html                                    lang="en">
<head>

<meta                    charset="utf-8"            />
<title>Draw two rectangles on the canvas</title>
<style>

canvas{
border:1px             solid                  gray;
}
</style>
<script                                      async>
window.onload = init; // call init() once the
window        is        completely         loaded
function                                   init(){
// #1 - get reference to <canvas> element
var canvas = document.querySelector('canvas');

 // #2 - get reference to the drawing context
and       drawing       API      var       ctx      =
canvas.getContext('2d');
```

```
// #3 - all fill operations are now in red ctx.fillStyle
=                                                      'red';
// #4 - fill a 100x100 rectangle at x=0,y=0
ctx.fillRect(0,0,100,100);

// #5 - all fill operations are now in green
ctx.fillStyle              =              'green';
// #6 - fill a 50x50 rectangle at x=25,y=25
ctx.fillRect(25,25,50,50);

}
</script>
</head>
<body>
<canvas width=300 height=200>Your browser
does not support canvas.</canvas> </body>
</html>
```

This example looks like this:

Meta Information

Meta tags in HTML documents provide useful information about the document including a description, keywords, author, dates of modifications and around 90 other fields. This topic covers the usage and purpose of these tags.

Section 33.1: Page Information
application-name

Giving the name of the Web application that the page represents.
<meta name="application-name" content="OpenStreetMap"**>**
If it's not a Web application, the application-name meta tag must not be used.
author
Set the author of the page:
<meta name="author" content="Your Name"**>**
Only one name can be given.
description
Set the description of the page:
<meta name="description" content="Page Description"**>**

The description meta tag can be used by various search engines while indexing your web page for searching purpose. Usually, the description contained within the meta tag is the short summary that shows up under the page/website's main title in the search engine results. Google usually uses only the first 20-25 words of your description.

generator

<meta name="generator" content="HTML Generator 1.42"**>**

Identifies one of the software packages used to generate the document. Only to be used for pages where the markup is automatically generated.

keywords

Set keywords for search engines (comma-separated):

<meta name="keywords" content="Keyword1, Keyword2"**>**

The keywords meta tag is sometimes used by search engines to know the search query which is relevant to your web page. As a rule of thumb, it is probably a good idea to not add too many words, as most search engines that use this meta tag for indexing will only index the first ~20 words. Make sure that you put the most important keywords first.

Section 33.2: Character Encoding

The charset attribute specifies the character encoding for the HTML document and needs to be a valid character encoding (examples include windows1252, ISO8859-2, Shift_JIS, and UTF8). UTF8 (Unicode) is the most widely used and should be used for any new project.

\<meta charset="UTF-8"**> \<meta** charset="ISO-8859-1"**>**

All browsers have always recognized the **\<meta** charset> form, but if you for some reason need your page to be valid HTML 4.01, you can use the following instead:

\<meta http-equiv="content-type" content="text/html; charset=UTF-8"**> \<meta** http-equiv="content-type" content="text/html; charset=ISO-8859-1"**>** See also the Encoding Standard, to view all available character encoding labels that browsers recognize.

Section 33.3: Robots

The robots attribute, supported by several major search engines, controls whether search engine spiders are allowed to index a page or not and whether they should follow links from a page or not.

\<meta name="robots" content="noindex"**>** This example instructs all search engines to not show the page in search results. Other allowed values are:

Value/Directive all

noindex
nofollow
follow

noarchive
nocache
nosnippet

noodp

notranslate
noimageindex

unavailable_after [RFC850 date/time]

Meaning
Default. Equivalent to index, follow. See note below.
Do not index the page at all.
Do not follow the links on this page
The links on the page can be followed. See note below.
Equivalent to noindex, nofollow.
Do not make a cached version of this page available in search results. Synonym of noarchive used by some bots such as Bing.
Do not show a snippet of this page in search results.
Do not use metadata of this page from the Open Directory project for titles or snippets in search results.
Do not offer translations of this page in search results.
Do not index images on this page.
Do not show this page in search results after the

157

specified date/time. The date/time must be specified in the RFC 850 format.

Note: Explicitly defining index and/or follow, while valid values, is not necessary as pretty much all search engines will assume they are allowed to do so if not explicitly prevented from doing so. Similar to how the robots.txt file operates, search engines generally only look for things they are *not allowed* to do. Only stating things a search engine isn't allowed to do also prevents accidentally stating opposites (such as index, ..., noindex) which not all search engines will treat in the same way.

Section 33.4: Social Media

Open Graph is a standard for metadata that extends the normal information contained within a site's head markup. This enables websites such as Facebook to display deeper and richer information about a website in a structured format. This information is then automatically displayed when users share links to websites containing OG metadata on Facebook.

Facebook / Open Graph

```
<meta                    property="fb:app_id"
content="123456789">
 <meta                    property="og:url"
```

```
content="https://example.com/page.html">
<meta property="og:type" content="website">
<meta property="og:title" content="Content Title">
<meta property="og:image" content="https://example.com/image.jpg">
<meta property="og:description" content="Description Here">
<meta property="og:site_name" content="Site Name">
<meta property="og:locale" content="en_US">
<meta property="article:author" content="">
<!-- Facebook: https://developers.facebook.com/docs/sharing/webmasters#markup --> <!-- Open Graph: http://ogp.me/ -->
```

Facebook Open Graph Markup Open Graph protocol

Facebook / Instant Articles
```
<meta charset="utf-8">
<meta property="op:markup_version" content="v1.0">
<!-- The URL of the web version of your article -> 
<link rel="canonical" href="http://example.com/article.html">
<!-- The style to be used for this article ->
<meta property="fb:article_style" content="myarticlestyle">
```
Facebook Instant Articles: Creating Articles Instant Articles: Format Reference

Twitter uses its own markup for metadata. This metadata is used as information to control how tweets are displayed when they contain a link to the site.

Twitter

```
<meta name="twitter:card" content="summary">
<meta name="twitter:site" content="@site_account">
<meta name="twitter:creator" content="@individual_account">
<meta name="twitter:url" content="https://example.com/page.html">
<meta name="twitter:title" content="Content Title">
<meta name="twitter:description" content="Content description less than 200 characters"> <meta name="twitter:image" content="https://example.com/image.jpg">
```

Twitter Cards: Getting Started Guide Twitter Card Validator

Google+ / Schema.org

```
<link href="https://plus.google.com/+YourPage" rel="publisher">
<meta itemprop="name" content="Content Title">
<meta itemprop="description" content="Content description less than 200 characters"> <meta
```

itemprop="image"
content="https://example.com/image.jpg">

Section 33.5: Mobile Layout Control
Common mobile-optimized sites use the **<meta** name="viewport"> tag like this: **<meta** name="viewport" content="width=device-width, initial-scale=1"> The viewport element gives the browser instructions on how to control the page's dimensions and scaling based on the device you are using.

In the above example, content="width=device-width means that the browser will render the width of the page at the width of its own screen. So if that screen is 480px wide, the browser window will be 480px wide. initialscale=1 depicts that the initial zoom (which is 1 in this case, means it does not zoom).

Below are the attributes this tag supports:
Attribute   **Description**
The width of the virtual viewport of the device.width Values1: devicewidth or the actual width in pixels, like 480

The height of the virtual viewport of the device. height Values2: deviceheight or the actual width in pixels, like 600 initial-scaleThe initial zoom when the page is

161

loaded. 1.0 does not zoom. minimum-scaleThe minimum amount the visitor can zoom on the page. 1.0 does not zoom. maximum-scaleThe maximum amount the visitor can zoom on the page. 1.0 does not zoom. Allows the device to zoom in and out. Values are yes or no. If set to no, the user is not able to zoom user-scalable in the webpage. The default is yes. Browser settings can ignore this rule.

Notes:

1 The width property can be either specified in *pixels* (width=600) or by *device-width* (width=devicewidth) which represents the physical width of the device's screen.
2 Similarly, the height property can be either specified in pixels (height=600) or by deviceheight (height=deviceheight) which represents the physical height of the device's screen.

Section 33.6: Automatic Refresh

To refresh the page every five seconds, add this meta element in the head element:
<meta http-equiv="refresh" content="5"**>**

CAUTION! While this is a valid command, it is recommended that you do not use it because of its negative effects on user experience. Refreshing the page too often can cause it to become unresponsive, and often scrolls to the top of the page. If some information on the page needs to be updated continuously, there are much better ways to do that by only refreshing a portion of a page.

Section 33.7: Phone Number Recognition

Mobile platforms like iOS automatically recognize phone numbers and turn them into tel: links. While the feature is very practical, the system sometimes detects ISBN codes and other numbers as telephone numbers. For mobile Safari and some other WebKit-based mobile browsers to turn off automatic phone number recognition and formatting, you need this meta tag:

`<meta name="format-detection" content="telephone=no">`

Section 33.8: Automatic redirect

Sometimes your webpage needs a automatic redirect.

For example, to redirect to example.com after 5 seconds:

`<meta http-equiv="refresh" content="5;url=https://www.example.com/" />`

This is line will send you to the designated website (in this case example.com after 5 seconds.

If you need to change the time delay before a

redirect, simply changing the number right before your ;url= will alter the time delay.

Section 33.9: Web App

You can set up your web app or website to have an application shortcut icon added to a device's homescreen, and have the app launch in full-screen "app mode" using Chrome for Android's "Add to homescreen" menu item. Below meta tag(s) will open web app in full-screen mode (without address bar). Android Chrome

<meta name="mobile-web-app-capable" content="yes"**>**

IOS

<meta name="apple-mobile-web-app-capable" content="yes"**>**

You can also set color for status bar and address bar in meta tag. Android Chrome

<meta name="theme-color" content="black"**>** IOS

<meta name="apple-mobile-web-app-status-bar-style" content="black"**>**

Marking up computer code

Section 34.1: Block with <pre> and <code>

If the formatting (white space, new lines, indentation) of the code matters, use the pre element in combination with the code element:

164

```
<pre>
<code>
x                        =                        42
if x == 42:

    print      "x      is      ...      ...      42"
</code>
</pre>
```

You still have to escape characters with special meaning in HTML (like < with <), so for *displaying* a block of HTML code (**<p>**This is a paragraph.**</p>**), it could look like this:

```
<pre>
<code>
&lt;p>This is a paragraph.&lt;/p> </code>

</pre>
```

Section 34.2: Inline with <code>

If a sentence contains computer code (for example, the name of an HTML element), use the code element to mark it up:
<p>The **<code>**a**</code>** element creates a hyperlink.**</p>**

Marking-up Quotes

Section 35.1: Inline with <q>

The **q element** can be used for a quote that is part   of   a   sentence:

```html
<p>She wrote <q>The answer is 42.</q> and everyone agreed.</p>
```

Quotation marks

Version ≤ 4.01

Quotation marks should not be added. User agents should (in HTML 4.01) resp. must (in HTML 4.0) render them automatically.

Version = 5

Quotation marks must not be added. User agents will render them automatically.

Source URL (cite attribute)

The **cite attribute** can be used to reference the URL of the quoted source:

```html
<p>She wrote <q cite="http://example.com/blog/hello-world">The answer is 42.</q> and everyone agreed.</p>
```

Note that browsers typically don't show this URL, so if the source is relevant, you should add a hyperlink (a element) in addition.

Section 35.2: Block with <blockquote>

The **blockquote element** can be used for a (block-level) quote:

```html
<blockquote>
<p>The answer is 42.</p>
</blockquote>
```

Source URL (cite attribute)

The **cite attribute** can be used to reference the URL of the quoted source:

```
<blockquote cite="http://example.com/blog/hello-world">
 <p>The answer is 42.</p>
</blockquote>
```

Note that browsers typically don't show this URL, so if the source is relevant, you should add a hyperlink (a element) in addition (see the section *Citation/Attribution* about where to place this link).

Citation/Attribution

Version ≤ 4.01

The citation/attribution should not be part of the blockquote element:

```
<blockquote cite="http://example.com/blog/hello-world">
 <p>The answer is 42.</p>
</blockquote>
<p>Source: <cite><a href="http://example.com/blog/hello-world" rel="external">Hello World</a></cite></p>
```

You can add a div element to group the quote and the citation, but it exists no way to associate them semantically.

The **cite element** can be used for the reference of the quoted source (but not for the author name).

Version   =   5

The citation/attribution (e.g., the hyperlink giving the source URL) can be inside the blockquote, but in that case it must be within a cite element (for in-text attributions) or a footer element:

```html
<blockquote cite="http://example.com/blog/hello-world">
 <p>The       answer       is       42.</p>
 <footer>

 <p>Source:                 <cite><a href="http://example.com/blog/hello-world" rel="external">Hello    World</a></cite></p>
 </footer>
 </blockquote>
```

The **cite element** can be used for the reference of the quoted source, or for the name of the quote's author.

Tabindex
Value Meaning

negative element will be focusable, but it should not be reachable via sequential keyboard navigation

0

element will be focusable and reachable through keyboard sequential navigation, but it's relative order is defined by the platform convention

positive element must be focusable and accessible via sequential keyboard navigation; it's relative order will be defined by the attribute value: the sequential follow the increasing number of the tabindex

Section 36.1: Add an element to the tabbing order

<div

tabindex="0">Some button**</div>**

Note: Try to use a native HTML button or an a tag where appropriate.

Section 36.2: Remove an element from the tabbing order

<button

tabindex="-1">This button will not be reachable by tab**</button>**

The element will be removed from the tabbing order but will still be focusable.

Section 36.3: Define a custom tabbing order (not recommended)

<div

tabindex="2">Second**</div>**

<div tabindex="1">First**</div>**

Positive values will insert the element at the tabbing order position of its respective value. Elements without preference (i.e. tabindex="0" or native elements such as button and a) will be appended after those with preference.

Positive values are **not recommended** as they disrupt the expected behavior of tabbing and might confuse people who rely on screenreaders. Try to create a natural order by rearranging your DOM structure.

Global Attributes

Attribute Description class Defines one or more class names for an element. See Classes and IDs. contenteditableSets whether the content of an element can be edited. contextmenu dir draggable hidden id

lang

spellcheck style tabindex

title

translate

Defines a context menu shown when a user right-clicks an element.

170

Sets the text direction for text within an element.
Sets whether an element can be dragged.
Hides an element not currently in use on the page.
Defines a unique identifier for an element. See Classes and IDs.

Defines the language of an element's content and its text attribute values. See Content Languages.

Sets whether to spell/grammar check the content of an element.
Defines a set of inline CSS styles for an element.
Sets the order in which elements on a page are navigated by the tab keyboard shortcut.

Defines additional information about an element, generally in the form of tooltip text on mouseover.
Defines whether to translate the content of an element.

Section 37.1: Contenteditable Attribute
<p
contenteditable**>This** is an editable paragraph.**</p>**
Upon clicking on the paragraph, the content of it can be edited similar to an input text field.
When the contenteditable attribute is not set on an element, the element will inherit it from

its parent. So all child text of a content editable element will also be editable, but you *can* turn it off for specific text, like so:

```
<p                          contenteditable>
This      is     an     editable     paragraph.
<span     contenteditable="false">But     not
this.</span>

</p>
```

Note that an uneditable text element inside an editable element will still have a text cursor as inherited from its parent as well.

HTML 5 Cache

Section 38.1: Basic Example of HTML5 cache
this is our index.html file

```
<!DOCTYPE                html                >
<html              manifest="index.appcache">
<body>

<p                            Content</p>
</body>
</html>
```

then we will create index.appcache file with below   codes
CACHE   MANIFEST   index.html

write those files that you want to be cached load index.html then go for offline mode and reload the tab **Note:** The two files must be in the same folder in this example

HTML Event Attributes

Section 39.1: HTML Form Events
Events triggered by actions inside a HTML form (applies to almost all HTML elements, but is most used in form elements):

Attribute	Description
onblur	Fires the moment that the element loses focus
onchange	Fires the moment when the value of the element is changed
oncontextmenu	Script to be run when a context menu is triggered
onfocus oninput oninvalid onreset onsearch onselect onsubmit	Fires the moment when the element gets focus
	Script to be run when an element gets user input
	Script to be run when an element is invalid
	Fires when the Reset button in a form is clicked
	Fires when the user writes something in a search field (for <input="search">)
	Fires after some text has been selected in an element
	Fires when a form is submitted

Section 39.2: Keyboard Events
Attribute Description

onkeydown Fires when a user is pressing a key
onkeypress Fires when a user presses a key
onkeyup Fires when a user releases a key

Character Entities

Section 40.1: Character Entities in HTML

Many symbols and special characters are required while developing a web page in html, but as we know that sometimes the use of characters directly may interfere with the actual html code which have certain characters reserved and also certain characters being not available on keyboard. Thus, to avoid the conflict and at same time to be able to use different symbols in our code w3 org provides us with 'Character Entities'.

Character Entities are predefined with 'Entity Name' - &entity_name; and 'Entity Number' - &entity_number; so we need to use either of the two for the required symbol to be rendered on   our   page.
The list of few Character Entities can be found at   https://dev.w3.org/html5/html-author/charref

A simple example with the use of character

entity for 'magnifying glass' :
<input type="text" placeholder=" 🔍
Search"**/>**

which renders as

Q Search

Section 40.2: Common Special Characters

Some character may be reserved for HTML and cannot be used directly as it may obstruct the actual HTML codes. For example, trying to display the left and right angle brackets (<>) in the source code may cause unexpected results in the output. Similarly, white spaces as written in the source code may not display as expected in the output HTML. Some, like ☎ are not available in the ASCII character set.

For this purpose, character entities are created. These are of the form &entity_name; or &entity_number;. The following are some of the available HTML entities.

Character	Description	Entity Name	Entity Number
" "	non-breaking space		
"<"	less than	&lt;	&#60;
">"	greater than	&gt;	&#62;
"&"	ampersand	&amp;	&#38;
"—"	em dash	&mdash;	&#8212;
"–"	en dash	&ndash;	&#8211;

175

"©"	copyright	&copy;	&#169;
"®"	registered trademark®	&#174;
"™"	trademark	&trade;	&#8482;
"☎" phone ☎ ☎

Thus, to write
© **2016 Stack Exchange Inc.**
the following HTML code is used:
****© 2016 Stack Exchange Inc.****

ARIA

Section 41.1: role="presentation"
An element whose implicit native role
semantics will not be mapped to the
accessibility API.

<div style="float:left;">Some content on the
left.**</div>**
 <div style="float:right;">Some content on the
right**</div>**
 <div role="presentation"
style="clear:both;">**</div>** <!-- Only used to clear
floats ->

Section 41.2: role="alert"
 A message with important, and usually time-
sensitive, information.
 <div role="alert" aria-live="assertive">Your
session will expire in 60 seconds.**</div>**

Note that I've included both role="alert" and aria-live="assertive" at the same time. These are synonymous attributes, but some screen readers only support one or the other. By using both simultaneously we therefore maximize the chances that the live region will function as expected.

Source - Heydon Pickering
'Some practical ARIA examples'

Section 41.3: role="alertdialog"
A type of dialog that contains an alert message, where initial focus goes to an element within the dialog.

```
<div role="alertdialog">
<h1>Warning</h1>
<div role="alert">Your session will expire in 60 seconds.</div>

</div>
```

Section 41.4: role="application"
A region declared as a web application, as opposed to a web document. In this example, the application is a simple calculator that might add two numbers together.

```
<div                    role="application">
<h1>Calculator</h1>
<input id="num1" type="text"> + <input
id="num2"    type="text">    =    <span
id="result"></span>

</div>
```

Section 41.5: role="article"
 A section of a page that consists of a
composition that forms an independent
part of a document, page, or site.
Setting an ARIA role and/or aria-*
attribute that matches the default
implicit ARIA semantics is unnecessary
and is not recommended as these
properties are already set by the
browser.

```
<article>
<h1>My first article</h1> <p>Lorem
ipsum...</p>

</article>
```
 You would use role=article on non-
semantic elements (not recommended,
invalid)

```html
<div                          role="article">
 <h1>My first article</h1>  <p>Lorem ipsum...</p>

</div>
```
W3C Entry for role=article

Section 41.6: role="banner"
A region that contains mostly site-oriented content, rather than page-specific content.
```html
<div                          role="banner">
 <h1>My Site</h1>

<ul>
 <li><a          href="/">Home</a></li>
 <li><a          href="/about">About</a></li>
 <li><a href="/contact">Contact</a></li>

</ul>
</div>
```

Section 41.7: role="button"
An input that allows for user-triggered actions when clicked or pressed. `<button role="button">Add</button>`

179

Section 41.8: role="cell"
A cell in a tabular container.
 \<table\>
 \<thead\>

\<!--   etc   -\>
 \</thead\>
 \<tbody\>

\<td   role="cell"**\>**95**\</td\>**
 \<td   role="cell"**\>**14**\</td\>**
 \<td role="cell"**\>**25**\</td\>**

 \</tbody\>
  \</table\>

Section 41.9: role="checkbox"
 A checkable input that has three possible
values: true, false, or mixed.

\<p\>
 \<input type="checkbox" role="checkbox" aria-
checked="false"**\>** I agree to the terms

 \</p\>

Section 41.10: role="columnheader"
 A cell containing header information for a
column.

```
<table                             role="grid">
<thead>

<tr>
<th       role="columnheader">Day      1</th>
<th       role="columnheader">Day      2</th>
<th role="columnheader">Day 3</th>

</tr>
</thead>
<tbody>

<!--              etc              ->
</tbody>
<table>
```

Section 41.11: role="combobox"
A presentation of a select; usually similar to a textbox where users can type ahead to select an option, or type to enter arbitrary text as a new item in the list. **<input** type="text" role="combobox" aria-expanded="false"**>** Typically, you would use JavaScript to build the rest of the typeahead or list select functionality.

Section 41.12: role="complementary"
A supporting section of the document, designed to be complementary to the main content at a similar level in the DOM hierarchy, but remains meaningful when separated from

the main content.
```
<div role="complementary">
<h2>More Articles</h2>

<ul>
<!-- etc -->
</ul>
</div>
```

Section 41.13: role="contentinfo"

Conclusion

Congratulations on making it to the end. You now have the skills to view a websites source code, and create your own. We have covered how to create, save, and view an HTML5 document, as well as format it properly.

Practice these skills and continue to research materials that will help you add more and more advanced features, until you can practically create a website in your sleep :)

Creating a website is a worthy goal. Long gone are the days when the internet was used only by the government and universities. Today thousands upon thousands of individuals make their voices heard over the internet through their blogs and websites. With the skills you have learned you can now create a website and share your own thoughts and feelings, products and services, and in time can even generate cash from a well-established website.

The skills you have learned interlock and you can easily become quite skilled by observing the source code of other websites and mimicking their methods, as well as using intuition and logic to combine the code in various ways until the result pleases you.

Before going live with a website, start small and dream big. Type out your headers, and your paragraphs and save them page by page until your content is substantial and will grab the attention of your intended audience. Once you feel you are ready, take a deep breath and go for it. Create your own space online and reap the rewards. Be patient, diligent, and hardworking. Create new content each day, never stop learning and you will be amazed at how far you took your first simple website as it grows more sophisticated and powerful beast.